How To Find Your Soulmate

Pragmatic Guidance for Discovering and Nurturing a Lasting, Ideal Romantic Partnership

(The person you are destined to love may be closer than you anticipate)

Herman Thomas

TABLE OF CONTENT

Desirable Attributes To Look For In A Life Partner 1

The Perception You Have Is Not An Accurate Representation Of Reality.. 9

The Threshold Matrix................................ 22

"Without Really Trying..." 43

Positive Outcomes Are Attained By Individuals Who Exercise Patience... 51

In Light Of One's Reverence For Christ, It Is Incumbent Upon Individuals To Yield To One Another... 70

What Are Effective Strategies For Capturing The Affection And Commitment Of A Male Partner In A Romantic Relationship? 80

Ensure That You Maintain Your Profile.......... 100

Discerning Your Desired Object Of Interest.. 112

What Is The Path To Reconnecting With One's Authentic Self?... 145

Acknowledge Your Preconceived Notion Of An Idealized Version Of Love And Free Yourself From Its Constraints. 157

Desirable Attributes To Look For In A Life Partner

Prior to embarking on any relationship, it is inevitable that we will possess a multitude of expectations. We are aware of what we desire from establishing a strong partnership and fostering a healthy relationship. We possess a thorough understanding of the commitment we are undertaking and are well aware of the essential contributions required to meet the relationship's demands. However, it is worth noting that the most fulfilling relationships are characterized by their ability to consistently present delightful surprises.

Capable of consistently prioritizing your needs above their own.

Arguably, love can be considered unnatural. It compels us to prioritize the needs of another individual above our own, contrary to what is expected according to evolutionary principles. The inherent charm of a nurturing relationship lies in the establishment of such a strong bond that dependence on one another becomes a natural inclination, resulting in a sense of unity where the desires of our significant other are perceived as our own, transcending our individual needs.

Failure is likely if your partner fails to prioritize your needs above their own, and if you are unable to prioritize your partner's needs above your own. Naturally, we cannot consistently prioritize the needs of our partners above our own; after all, we are fallible beings. However, we can endeavor to demonstrate our profound love for them by making sacrifices, ensuring their needs are met while prioritizing their desires.

Determination

The resolute drive of an individual to forge their own prosperous trajectory in life will yield a positive impact on the relationship. The presence of personal resolve establishes a harmonious rhythm within the partnership, as long as both individuals motivate and encourage one another towards their individual aspirations. Choose a partner who ardently endeavors to ensure a prosperous existence for the both of you, while concurrently motivating you to fulfill your purpose in life.

Expose you to a novel dimension of existence - unveil a fresh perspective.

A life of immense value is one that is characterized by continuous exploration and revelation. Encountering novel opportunities is invigorating and provides fresh perspectives to anticipate. Furthermore, the perfect life partner will unveil to you an elevated perspective of existence - an aspect that was previously unbeknownst to your awareness. It is highly probable that the individual with whom you will ultimately share your life is the one who guides you towards a more refined manner of existence.

Self-care

The manner in which an individual behaves toward themselves is indicative of how they will conduct themselves towards you. If your partner engages in self-destructive behavior, how can you anticipate them to contribute positively to your growth and development? If individuals demonstrate a total disregard for their home, occupation, possessions, well-being, or personal presentation, it is probable that they will be incapable of providing you with the level of care that you desire and deserve. Seek an individual who conducts themselves in a responsible and considerate manner, so as to manifest such behavior towards yourself.

Commitment

Enduring relationships are the deeply gratifying connections we yearn for, as opposed to fleeting romances that have brief durations. It is imperative to have the assurance of a reliable and enduring companion, someone who is committed to nurturing a relationship indefinitely, and possesses a profound comprehension of the dedication, collaboration, and selflessness it entails. It is excessively uncomplicated to engage with an individual who abandons their commitments when confronted with adversity. It is indicative of a potential soulmate when one encounters a partner who not only articulates the inclination for enduring commitment, but also substantiates their assertions through tangible deeds.

Your soulmate exhibits unwavering loyalty and would never forsake you.

Life can be extremely challenging. It has the potential to cause significant distress. It may render the act of arising in the morning and conducting our daily affairs nearly unattainable. It has the potential to evoke negative emotions such as moodiness, unhappiness, stress, haste, anger, emotional instability, and fluctuating moods. However, this becomes of greater concern when one begins to share their life with another individual.

Are you capable of handling your partner during times of difficulty? Is your partner capable of managing and handling you? What is the excessive amount? These are inquiries that necessitate self-reflection. Loyalty holds significant value and plays a crucial role in fostering strong relationships.

At times, we experience a loss of self-control and descend into that downward spiral. Will your romantic partner remain by your side as you emerge from that difficult situation?

Both of you have a strong desire to lead remarkably similar lives.

During our younger years, we often neglect to give adequate consideration to the kind of lifestyles we aspire to adopt. Alternatively, we do not give significant consideration to the potential scenario where our personal aspirations may not align with the desires and aspirations of our partner.

Would you prefer a lifestyle of continuous travel or remaining in one place? Do you aspire to achieve great wealth or merely seek financial stability? Do you want kids? And how many? All of these decisions have an impact on various aspects of our lives.

Engaging in significant endeavors demands significant investment of time and effort. Given that we are in a reciprocal relationship, it is highly probable that both parties will experience some form of deprivation. Ideally, those matters ought not to carry immense significance to our partners, as their prominence would inevitably pave the way for grave consequences to befall upon us.

The Perception You Have Is Not An Accurate Representation Of Reality.

What perceptions do you hold when your gaze rests upon me?

Do you happen to observe an individual in his forties, with untidy hair, a father to two offspring, of English origin, or conceivably someone's significant other? Maybe I inadvertently interrupted your path on the roadway, and it is undeniable that I am no superior than an egocentric imbecile. Alternatively, perhaps you inadvertently misplaced your wallet, which I promptly retrieved and returned to you... symbolizing my considerate nature as an individual who spared you significant distress and inconvenience. The perceptions and beliefs regarding my identity are inconsequential, as they are mere illusions. I am not the person you perceive me to be; rather, I serve as a reflection of the inner aspects of your being.

Regrettably, we are all culpable of perceiving that which aligns with our desires. Consider your partner, for example; if you desire, you can embark on a endeavor to procure evidence suggesting their indifference towards you and their lack of genuine affection. Just as inevitably as the transition from day to night, the corpus of reinforcing evidence for this line of thinking will accrue steadily until you possess an unassailable argument that substantiates your assertion. Based on my personal observation and past encounters, I can affirm the veracity of this theory. However, it is worth noting that this theory also holds true in reverse. If one embarks upon a quest to ascertain the manifestation of affection and admiration from one's partner, the substantiation shall surface abundantly in every direction.

However, it is intriguing to ponder how the individual's identity remains unaltered, yet a diametrically opposed response to one's inquiry is obtained merely by modifying one's mindset. To put it concisely, the world you perceive is non-solid. It is a malleable construct of your own making, where your perception of reality can transfigure according to your will. I shall now proceed to provide a more detailed response without any further delay.

I desire for you to have a precise understanding of my identity. I do not possess the knowledge or the moral standing of a guru or a saint; indeed, I am quite far from attaining such status. Similarly to yourself, I peruse the writings of esteemed spiritual guides like Eckhart Tolle and Deepak Chopra, and am awe-inspired by the serene and harmonious nature of their existence. I am among those who contemplate existence; this aspect has been as much of a burden as it is a gift. Personally, I cannot readily embrace concepts or ideas that lack comprehensibility to me; I find it imperative to critically analyze and rationalize prevailing beliefs or norms. If I do not take action, the idea will persist as an untamed creature, unrestricted to wander and bring forth distress and chaos. Of course, this is an impossible mission because many of life's wonders and challenges must forever remain a mystery, and yet I continue to try first to understand them for myself and then share my hard fought comprehension with the world.

I have consistently offered guidance to individuals seeking weight loss, cautioning against relying on individuals deemed as 'experts' solely based on their naturally slender physique. I strongly recommend that you refrain from following the weight loss guidance offered by your overweight general practitioner or any other healthcare professionals who are overweight. If you desire to shed a substantial amount of weight, seek guidance from an individual who has endured a similar journey and successfully navigated the challenges. I am not present in order to divulge the details of my consistently ideal and affectionate relationships, nor to admonish you for not meeting my impeccable criteria. That would all be an exaggerated falsehood of significant magnitude. I am unable to assert that I have consistently assumed the role of a mediator without ever taking on the role of an aggressor. I must confess that demonstrating selfless love has not always been my approach towards my significant others throughout my life.

When I make the determination to embark on the task of authoring a book, I do so exclusively after experiencing numerous and repetitive setbacks in comprehending the subject matter. Prior to attaining expertise in overcoming alcohol dependency and producing the book 'Alcohol Lied to Me', my area of expertise extended to consistently struggling to cease alcohol consumption for a duration exceeding ten years. For a decade, I dedicated my efforts towards managing and moderating my alcohol consumption until a pivotal moment revealed the elusive solution. Since then,

I have successfully treated more than 50,000 individuals afflicted with severe alcohol addiction. I could chastise myself for not embarking on this trajectory earlier, but such self-reproach would serve no purpose. The numerous instances of failure have imparted valuable lessons and the accumulation of these experiences has bestowed me with the understanding to conceive an effective solution.

Presently, I find myself engaged in the authorship of a book centered around cultivating extraordinary and affectionate relationships. I find myself in possession of an abundance of knowledge, painstakingly acquired, just like all my other books. Indeed, it is indeed accurate that I possess extensive expertise in the realm of fostering relationships that lack affection and influence, hence making it highly beneficial for you to lend me your ear. Rest assured that there exists a perfect balance and mutual interdependence between the contrasting aspects of my persona. Much like the inability to comprehend the sensation of heat without the contrasting sensation of cold for reference, it holds true in this situation as well. I can assert that my accumulation of wisdom, which enables me to impart this knowledge to you today, is directly attributable to the multitude of failures I have experienced throughout my life.

If your aspirations encompass locating an ideal life partner, resolving marital difficulties, reconciling familial discord, fostering improved rapport with your superior, or simply establishing acquaintances, it is certain that the fundamental principles delineated within the pages of this book will furnish invaluable assistance.

Principle 1: The perceived visual stimuli do not accurately reflect reality.
Principle 2: Life operates on the principle of cause and effect, where one's actions invariably result in corresponding consequences.

Concept 3: The only course of action available is to engage in cleaning tasks.

These three principles will prove beneficial... Provided you can temporarily set aside any skepticism or distrust that might reside within your conscious mind. If you are able to wholeheartedly adopt and put into practice the principles outlined in this book, you will witness profound and constructive transformations in all of your interpersonal connections.

Let us temporarily set aside the complex notion that the perception of others is merely an illusion, and instead primarily focus on the subject of human motivation, exploring the factors that drive individuals to act and react in certain ways. It is often a common tendency to view oneself through a positive filter, perceiving all actions as entirely rational and logical. Nevertheless, it is common for us to discard our subjective perspectives and classify the actions of others (which may be indistinguishable from our own) using derogatory terms such as 'selfish', 'cruel', 'malicious', or a plethora of other unfavorable descriptors. The fundamental truth is that each one of us is grappling with existence to the best of our abilities, employing the resources at our disposal. The behavior of your boss or partner, no matter how unpleasant it may seem, holds little significance. No individual possesses the intention of intentionally inflicting anguish upon others without reason. Their actions, though capable of causing harm and offense, are seldom motivated by an intentional desire to do so.

Bullies engage in their hurtful behavior not out of sadistic pleasure, but rather as a manifestation of their inner insecurities, driven by their limited repertoire for coping with their own deep-seated fears. Your former partner did not engage in infidelity with the intention of causing you harm, but rather their actions were influenced by an internal dialogue fueled by their own vulnerable ego. This principle extends to individuals of all walks of life, encompassing both those who exhibit discourteous behavior such as cutting you off on the roadway and even the leaders of entire nations. No political leader in recorded history has ever directed their nation to engage in armed conflict with neighboring countries (resulting in the untimely demise of numerous innocent individuals) solely driven by malevolence. All individuals in question conducted their actions under the conviction that their endeavors were advantageous for their respective communities. The heinous acts of mass genocide perpetrated by Saddam Hussein during his prolonged rule in Iraq were motivated by his adherence to the strict teachings of the Baathist party and his conviction as a Sunni Muslim that any deviation from a precise interpretation of the Koran posed a substantial threat to the wellbeing of the nation's populace. Until his final breath, Saddam steadfastly believed that every action he undertook was ultimately in the best interests of his people.

Even in instances involving serial killers, their actions are not motivated by a deliberate intent to perpetrate evil. They are reacting to discomfort and taking actions they consider suitable for alleviating it. When it comes to these remorseless perpetrators of violence, one could make the case that responsibility ought to be directed towards the parents rather than the individual who perpetrated the offenses. A substantial portion of individuals with severe mental disorders, whose actions of abuse, rape, and murder receive prominent media coverage, have experienced previous traumas and a lack of nurturing during their formative years. I am definitely not advocating for unrestricted leniency towards all individuals who have been found guilty, and I would be grateful if you or your family have had personal experiences of suffering due to someone similar to this. The mere notion of such an idea may be highly distressing to you. I endeavor solely to illustrate that all assessments regarding moral value or quality are extraordinarily subjective.

If a child who experienced regular physical abuse and never witnessed a single display of compassionate behavior proceeds to lead a life characterized by violence, causing harm and distress to others, who bears the ultimate responsibility?

Consider the conduct of leaders from Western nations. Just last week, the British media proudly announced that RAF airstrikes against ISIS militants in Syria resulted in the successful elimination of hundreds of individuals. The reported deaths of numerous (malevolent) individuals are largely viewed as inconsequential by the majority of individuals in Western societies. The prime minister, who issued the orders resulting in their deaths, is regarded as an individual making resolute choices amidst challenging conditions. However, do you believe that the individuals who lost their lives would refer to the British Prime Minister in a similar manner as their families? Naturally, they will regard him as a scheming, malevolent individual harboring intense animosity. The identical individual, engaging in identical actions, is given entirely divergent reputations depending on the observer's perspective.

The undeniable reality is that individuals seldom comport themselves in the manner we opt to designate them. In actuality, they are driven to behave in such a manner by the identical pair of psychological factors that exert influence over all individuals. There exist solely two states of consciousness that govern all human responses, specifically the sensations of gratification and anguish. All of our actions are driven by the pursuit of pleasure or the avoidance of pain. Regrettably, our efforts to accomplish the latter outweigh those invested in attaining the former.

Suffering is the most potent catalyst for human beings. This phenomenon elucidates why a considerable number of individuals, dissatisfied with their physical proportions, embark upon a dietary regimen, only to relinquish their quest prematurely after shedding a meager few pounds, failing to attain the desired physique that would bring them contentment. I refer to this process of taking action until the pain subsides but lacking the persistence to continue until reaching a state of pleasure as the threshold matrix.

The Threshold Matrix

Jenny gazes at her reflection in the mirror and notices the gradual emergence of an additional layer of adipose tissue encircling her midsection. She lets out a resigned sigh and gazes mournfully at the wardrobe replete with garments that no longer align with her physique. The individual's dissatisfaction stems from her physical weight and body size; however, she is currently unable to justify relinquishing the food she enjoys, which she associates with a lifestyle that she deems deserving. Based on her present mental assessment, she believes that the absence of gourmet meals, indulgent desserts, and occasional dining out on weekends will prove to be a more disagreeable experience than her current dissatisfaction with her physical appearance.

The following day, an event of significant impact occurs at her workplace, causing a substantial shift in her perspective. As she disembarks from the elevator and proceeds towards her designated work area, she comes to an abrupt halt and lingers momentarily prior to rounding the corner. Upon hearing her name being mentioned in conversation, she inclines her head slightly, attentively attending to the discourse at hand. A new intern is inquiring about the identity of Jenny Taylor with a member of the sales team, as the intern needs to make a delivery at her desk. The sales representative, who is hurriedly leaving for a client meeting, exclaims while glancing back, "Please attend to cubicle 17, where you will find a distinguished lady with brown hair."

Jenny is astonished as she experiences the sensation of being struck across the face by the realization that her coworkers refer to her as 'the prominent lady' of the office. In my publication focused on weight loss, titled "Fat Guy Friday," I refer to this occurrence as a defining moment. This denotes a juncture at which the equilibrium between pleasure and pain experiences a dramatic shift. Abruptly, the distress arising from one's excessive weight and the resulting diminished self-perception is greatly magnified, surpassing the previously inconsequential constraints that hindered the individual from initiating any actions.

Taken aback by the unsettling revelation she has just stumbled upon, Jenny promptly discards her indulgent fried chicken lunch and embarks upon a strict dietary regimen. On her commute back from work, she makes a detour to the fitness center and enrolls herself in a yearly membership for the despised treadmill (although her dislike for the gym falls short of deterring her, unable to fully discount the persistent phrase 'larger woman, brunette'). Fitness centres often enter customers into contractual agreements of fixed duration, as they are aware that the individual's initial commitment is typically sustained for a relatively short period, ranging from six to eight weeks at most. Subsequently, you may find yourself vigorously requesting that they cease the monthly withdrawal of funds from your account. Dedicated patrons of fitness centers express discontent towards the month of January due to the congestion of treadmills and stationary bikes caused by individuals adhering to New Year's resolutions; fortunately, by the arrival of March, the majority of these individuals have ceased their attendance. Whilst it is highly likely that they continue to remit the club fees, it is worth noting that terminating a gym membership can be comparably challenging to dissolving a marital union.

The rabbit food serves as a substitute for the pizza, while Jenny Taylor diligently frequents the gym on a daily basis for an entire month. The salesman receives a minimum of twelve disapproving glances on a daily basis, as the reverberation of his depiction resounds within her psychologically injured consciousness. Commencing her mornings with a wholesome portion of diet cereal, opting for a salad during midday, and savoring a meal of gently cooked fish in the evening... until the day arrives when a pair of jeans that used to be snug effortlessly glides over her hips. A pleasant event for any individual watching their diet, the following day at her place of employment, upon returning in her slim attire, some of her coworkers take notice of her weight loss and express their approval in her direction. The motivational scales experience a shift as the discomfort associated with the defining moment subsides and diminishes its influence.

In approximately one week, Jenny has decided to indulge in the occasional indulgence and forgo attending the gym on days when she experiences slight fatigue. Within a month, she has developed a sense of dissatisfaction towards the $70 monthly deduction made by the fitness center from her account, perceiving it as an inadequate return on investment given the infrequent occasions when she manages to surpass the exit on the highway. It is only a matter of time before the suffering caused by denying oneself life's indulgences becomes more significant than the agony of that distant, defining incident. The weight gradually reverts back until the cycle initiates once more.

This phenomenon is commonly referred to as the yo-yo dieting cycle. It is observed that a significant majority of individuals, approximately 95%, who engage in a low-fat, calorie-restricted diet not only experience weight regain but also tend to gain an additional average of 2-5 pounds. Thin individuals may pass judgment upon these individuals and assign them various derogatory labels such as indolent or avaricious. However, the reality is that they are simply engaging in the same behavioral response as the rest of us - endeavoring to avoid experiencing distressing emotions.

Therefore, let us proceed to employ this principle in the context of the relationships in your life. Kindly allocate a moment of reflection to consider the individual with whom you are presently experiencing difficulty. It is of little consequence whether it is your adolescent daughter engendering disorder, your significant other failing to exhibit the affection and reverence you presently require, or your employer needlessly exacerbating the challenges of existence. Whilst contemplating on these individuals, reflect upon the designations that you have previously attributed to them. Maybe you have depicted your daughter as insubordinate, your partner as self-centered, or your boss as tyrannical. Please, kindly shut thy eyes and endeavor to envision the possibility of extricating thyself from thy corporeal vessel, assuming the role of an impartial observer peering upon thy interpersonal connection. Reflect upon a specific tumultuous moment with this individual and envision yourself as an observer hovering above the situation, witnessing the manner in which both parties are engaged and responding to one another.

Subsequently, set aside the use of labels and instead endeavor to discern the underlying motives that drive the behavior of the other individual. Please be mindful that this task is relatively straightforward, as it solely involves the consideration of two fundamental catalysts: pleasure and pain. If your daughter engages in vocal outbursts towards you and vehemently refuses to organize her living space, evaluate whether she displays a discernible sense of pleasure in engaging with you during this interaction. It is highly unlikely, and hence we must infer that she is being driven by pain as a result. It is possible that she is grappling with issues regarding her sense of identity, as she lacks clarity on her true self and the values she ought to uphold. The combination of this perplexity and an abundance of adolescent hormones is inflicting anguish upon her, and her sole aim is to distance herself from such emotional distress. Therefore, she is exhibiting hostility towards you and undermining your position of power. The issue of whether she is making the correct decision at present is immaterial to the task at hand. Rest assured that her intentions for engaging in conflict with you are not arbitrary or driven by a desire to cause harm. She is employing her chosen approach to distance herself from anguish, based on her beliefs. Although she could possibly be mistaken, it is imperative to reflect upon whether or not one has ever successfully prevailed in a debate by directly pointing out the other party's errors.

Please bear in mind that each of us is exerting maximum effort given the resources available to us. This does not imply that we should consistently exhibit the ability to consistently make judicious decisions; rather, it signifies that the majority of us are merely contending with life's challenges in a manner that appears most favorable at any particular instance.

Upon achieving the ability to disassociate oneself from the classifications and appraisals of one's ego. If you relinquish your efforts to forcibly elevate your relationship and instead release your grasp, you will observe a significant reduction in the occurrence of turmoil and anxiety in your life. Bear in mind, one's sense of self is particularly apprehensive about experiencing any form of loss. This does not solely pertain to the prospect of losing tangible possessions, but rather encompasses the broader concept of relinquishing both material and emotional assets, encompassing various mental states that one may mistakenly consider to be their own. If you are a parent, it is plausible that you hold the belief that you are entitled to the respect of your child, a notion that could indeed hold validity. However, the issue arises when one's ego becomes intertwined with this belief, as any disrespect shown by one's child can be seen as a personal affront, a theft of the very entity one holds as their own.

Cease your movement immediately, Craig.

Are you genuinely proposing that I should permit others to treat me however they please?

Do I lack the authority to express my own perspective?

Certainly not; there will inevitably arise occasions where it becomes necessary to take action in order to ensure the safety and well-being of oneself and one's familial unit. My point is that the possession of knowledge equates to empowerment. By abstaining from reacting to ego-related injuries, one will discover a noticeable reduction in the amount of stress and conflict encountered in life.

This exemplifies the use of strategic cognitive tactics, which I refer to as mental Judo...

Despite the debilitating car accident which claimed his left arm, a resilient and determined 10-year-old boy made the bold choice to embark on the study of judo.

The young lad commenced his training under the tutelage of a seasoned, venerable judo sensei hailing from Japan. The young lad was progressing admirably, hence his bewilderment arose as to why, subsequent to a trimester of instruction, the skilled instructor had solely imparted upon him a solitary maneuver. "Teacher," the boy eventually voiced, "Ought I not be acquiring additional techniques?" "Although this is the sole technique you have mastered, it is the sole technique you shall ever require," responded the instructor.

Despite not fully grasping the concept, yet maintaining faith in his instructor, the young boy persisted in his training. After the passage of several months, the sensei accompanied the young boy to his inaugural tournament. Unexpectedly, the young man effortlessly emerged victorious in his initial two contests. The third match presented greater challenges, however, subsequently, his adversary grew restless and made a hasty advance; the young individual skillfully employed their sole technique to secure victory in the match. Remain in awe of his triumph, the young lad had advanced to the finals.

On this occasion, his adversary possessed greater physical stature, strength, and a higher level of expertise. Temporarily, it seemed as though the young boy was outmatched. Fearing potential harm to the boy, the referee made the decision to call a time-out. He was on the verge of halting the match when the sensei interceded. Despite objections, the sensei firmly asserted, 'No, let him carry on.' Subsequently, as the competition recommenced, his adversary committed a pivotal error, carelessly neglecting his defense. Without delay, the young boy employed his maneuver to immobilize his opponent. The young lad emerged victorious in both the match and the tournament.

He was the champion. During the journey back, the young boy and his instructor diligently analyzed and evaluated every single maneuver executed throughout the matches. Subsequently, the young man mustered the bravery to inquire about his genuine concerns.

Excuse me, teacher, may I inquire as to how I emerged victorious in the tournament using merely a single technique?

The sensei responded that you emerged victorious for two primary factors. Primarily, you have nearly achieved proficiency in one of the most challenging throws within the realm of judo. Furthermore, the sole recognized countermeasure against that maneuver involves your adversary seizing hold of your left arm."

The most significant vulnerability of the boy has turned into his greatest asset.

Mental Judo is a strategic approach to interpersonal interactions whereby individuals effectively employ the momentum and energy of others to their advantage. When grappling with conflict, individuals often exhibit a heightened state of attentiveness directed towards their ego. Regardless of your awareness, your actions are inflicting pain upon them. They are experiencing great distress, as their sense of self is vehemently objecting to your attempt to appropriate something that belongs to them. Your spouse might perceive a sense of their personal autonomy being infringed upon due to your inclination for them to join your family over the weekend, instead of partaking in a round of golf alongside their companions. Your spouse might perceive that you have diminished the regard she deserves, as your lack of acknowledgement regarding her challenging work week. By refraining from reacting based on personal ego, you ameliorate the conflict.

Naturally, employing such a passive approach may result in a reduction of conflicts in your life; nevertheless, there lies a risk in failing to fulfill your own personal needs. In order to mitigate this risk, it is imperative to ensure effective communication and establish unambiguous boundaries. It is essential to effectively communicate your emotions to the other party in a nonconfrontational manner, while maintaining detachment from personal mental states, and clearly establish your boundaries. For instance, your adolescent son might exhibit an unwillingness to organize his living space, resorting to verbal outbursts and displays of frustration directed towards you. Previously, it is possible that you engaged in a verbal confrontation and reacted to his mistreatment by asserting your role as his parent. Through the application of mental judo, there is no necessity to retaliate, as one comprehends that the offensive conduct stems not from a personal grievance, but rather from a reaction to internal suffering. Nevertheless, it is not imperative for you to capitulate to his objections. You possess the capacity to articulately and composedly communicate the extent of your personal limits. No individual is granted the authority to violate the boundaries you have established for yourself, as these boundaries are deeply personal and integral to your ethical framework.

Synopsis: The first principle to manifest enchanting connections involves acknowledging the underlying reasons behind individuals' reactions, which may differ significantly from one's own anticipated response in such circumstances. Regardless of the actions or words of the 'other person', it should not be viewed as a personal matter. Please keep in mind that each of us is managing our lives to the best of our abilities, given the resources available to us.

"Without Really Trying..."

When discussing the concept of discovering one's soulmate effortlessly, I genuinely emphasize the aspect of not actively making an effort. This does not imply refraining from taking any form of action. Upon examining my narrative, it becomes evident that I did not have any intent to seek out my soulmate, or anyone else for that matter. The series of occurrences that transpired leading to our encounter was not coincidental. And indeed, in my perspective, these series of events were logically coherent as they transpired, they were inevitable!

As you may have started to infer, the underlying principle at play here is the Law of Attraction. I failed to fully grasp the significance of this law at that particular moment. However, it constitutes an intrinsic principle with far-reaching impact on all facets. It is evident that the idea in question is not a whimsical notion conjured by the New Age community. The Law of Attraction is founded upon the relationship between one's thoughts and emotions. The objects of your attention and the emotions you experience, consistently sustained, have the potential to materialize in your tangible surroundings.

How frequently have you contemplated individuals with whom you have had no contact for a considerable duration, only to encounter them within a brief span of time? Alternatively, it is possible that you harbored a particular desire and it manifested itself in your actuality. Each one of us has encountered such experiences, often without delving into the underlying rationale.

As we undergo the process of maturation, we are instilled with the knowledge of the significance of maintaining a positive mental outlook, often without fully comprehending its true significance. For more than two decades, I have been instructing individuals on metaphysical and spiritual principles. Through my extensive experience, I have come to understand that each day serves as a mirror, reflecting the thoughts and emotions that reside within me. We unwittingly employ the principles of the Law of Attraction in our daily lives. It can be likened to an inconspicuous background fan that escapes our conscious attention.

According to the principle of the Law of Attraction, it is suggested that phenomena of a similar nature tend to be drawn towards one another. Consider the instances in which you have experienced a positive state of mind; often, the events of your day seem to align with and reflect that positive mindset. Alternatively, you may find yourself waking up feeling irritable, and subsequently experiencing a series of unfortunate events throughout the day. Existence is not a haphazard progression of occurrences, but rather a methodical progression of occurrences determined by the energy encapsulating your thoughts, attitudes, and emotions. We may occasionally find ourselves disliking the course of events, yet these circumstances are determined by our cognitive and emotional perspectives.

The fundamental underpinning principle of life rests upon the concept of energy. According to scientific experts, physical entities are fundamentally composed of atomic structures, suggesting that their material nature may not be as straightforward as commonly perceived. All entities, in reality, consist of energy.

As stated in the literary work titled The Subtle Body: An Encylopedia to your Energetic Anatomy, it is posited that the human existence is encompassed by an intangible, vast expanse of energy, characterized by impeccable harmony, and imperceptible to the naked eye... All matter is comprised of this energy. Every individual cell exhibits electrical pulsations, while the physical body emits electromagnetic fields. The human physique constitutes a intricate energetic framework...

This assertion is in accordance with the opinions held by the esteemed figures of Albert Einstein and Nikola Tesla.

Every aspect of existence is a manifestation of the energy in our immediate environment. It is often claimed that "The mightiest force in the universe is the intellect-driven thought." Once we comprehend the capacity of our thoughts, emotions, and mindsets to shape our lives, an entirely revised trajectory for life emerges.

Once you acquire the ability to harmonize with your inherent creative energy, exertion becomes unnecessary. Typically, excessive effort tends to complicate matters. Despite the traditional upbringing that instills the belief in the correlation between diligent efforts and eventual success. I did not exert substantial effort in discovering my soulmate, and the same holds true for you. By comprehending and effectively employing the Law of Attraction, one can potentially experience increased ease in navigating through life. You have the potential to embody the essence of an artist, skillfully shaping the clay into an exquisite masterpiece.

If you allow events to progress naturally, everything will transpire flawlessly. Upon introspection of my narrative, it becomes apparent that I did not actively endeavor to actualize any events; instead, the cosmos evolved in response to the energy I had projected. The singular subject which piqued my keen interest prior to relocating to Springfield solely coincided with the specific topic being taught in a workshop by Linda and Brenda. Consequently, it prompted me to discover my soul mate.

Indeed, although I took necessary measures to arrive at that point, I simply found myself compelled to address the circumstances that were unfolding before me. It was solely and straightforwardly the compelling essence of the universe in operation. Like attracts like. The greater your fervor towards a certain matter, the more swiftly it manifests in your life. I possessed great enthusiasm and keenness for a particular matter. The remainder appeared to have been handled effortlessly. Life can be an enjoyable journey when you embrace it!

Positive Outcomes Are Attained By Individuals Who Exercise Patience.

Oh, I apologize, but are you suggesting that I should exercise - forgive my hesitance in uttering it - an elevated level of forbearance?

You got it, girlfriend!

However, I have patiently awaited for a significant amount of time, and regrettably remain unmarried even at the age of thirty-five.

Welcome to my world. I encountered Jerry for the first time when I reached the age of thirty-four and a half. Subsequent to this meeting, I entered into wedlock just nine months later. I comprehend the sense of exasperation that arises from the anticipation of waiting, the uncertainty surrounding the arrival of your destined partner, and the possibility of enduring a solitary and desolate existence.

However, I can affirm with complete assurance that the patience invested in our relationship was undeniably worthwhile.

In order to avoid any misconception regarding my strict adherence to rules, it is imperative that I elucidate upon the tumultuous narrative of my formative years, which bestowed upon me the sagacity I possess today with regards to the significance of patience. During the interim between my college years, I found myself faced with a sense of ennui during one summer. While employed in a dining establishment, I encountered an individual named Mark.

He bore a nineteen-year seniority over me, a practitioner of tobacco indulgence and a subscriber to alcoholic patterns. It would later come to my knowledge that he engaged in sexual relationships with any willing woman he encountered. (I am pleased to declare that I was not among those women.) More on that later.)

Initially, I was inclined to disregard him. He wasn't even handsome. However, he was the initial individual to bestow upon me any semblance of affection, ultimately proving himself to be a paragon of endearment - a fact of great significance since I had been bereft of such displays of tenderness - and he possessed exceptional skill in playing the piano.

I developed feelings for him due to these reasons, coupled with the fact that he possessed exceptional mastery in the art of emotional manipulation.

Rather than succumbing to my initial instincts toward him, which urged caution and distance, I consciously disregarded those feelings due to my aversion to solitude and monotony. I had been prepared to enter into a romantic partnership with a gentleman for a duration of several years, contemplating that should he develop feelings for me, I would be able to influence a positive transformation within him whereby all his personal challenges would cease to exist.

I had no desire to endure any delay.

The relationship ultimately dissolved a few years later upon my discovery that he had been engaging in an intimate and social manner with a young woman in her twenties whilst I was attending college elsewhere. Furthermore, he had extended a proposal of marriage to both of us simultaneously, on the exact date.

I am not cognizant of the precise content of her statement, however, my response entailed advising to refrain from consuming alcoholic beverages in the first instance.

Allow me to present a revelation to you: it is unlikely that he will embark on his journey towards sobriety before others. It is imperative that you exercise patience and await the company of an individual who abstains from indulging in activities such as drinking, promiscuity, gambling, or any other objectionable behaviors that do not align with your personal standards for a partner. Indeed, it is possible that your significant other could be the charming colleague who indulges in cocaine on a nightly basis. However, it will also transpire that the present moment is not opportune for establishing any kind of connection or association with him. The moment shall arise upon his attainment of sobriety and reformation.

Mark's infidelity had such a profound impact on me that it caused me to harbor animosity towards men for the subsequent nine-year period. Had I not been in such haste when I was twenty years old, I would have been spared immense agony, sorrow, and anxiety. It is my sincere aspiration that through the perusal of my narrative, you may encounter a measure of solace bestowed upon you by the divine, thus prompting you to cease your active pursuit of a romantic partner and commence the practice of exhibiting patience.

What does it resemble?

Pray.

Pray to the Lord for assistance during periods of solitude. Moreover, it would be advantageous to allocate a portion of your leisure time each day to engage in prayer, specifically dedicating it to intercede for a multitude of individuals. Upon engaging in this practice for several consecutive days, it is highly likely that you will experience an increase in emotional investment towards the individuals for whom you are offering prayers. There is truly no substitute for cultivating genuine empathy and concern for others, as it effectively redirects one's attention away from personal preoccupations.

When directing your prayers towards your longing for a kindred spirit, beseech the divine for his presence and entreat that both of you shall cross paths in accordance with the impeccable timing of the divine will. Allow me to be forthright: had I encountered Jerry when he weighed 280 pounds (considering his modest height of only five-foot-seven) and during a phase where my sentiment towards men was less favorable, there would have been no room for any sort of connection between us.

Nothing. I regret employing an elitist tone, but individuals with a larger physique do not appeal to me.

Moreover, should you earnestly seek divine intervention for the precise orchestration of events, there is a reduced inclination to assert authority and regain command.

Maybe. We are inclined to believe. ;)

Get involved.

There exist numerous community and social organizations which span a wide range, encompassing religious fellowships and Meet-Up groups oriented towards various interests and beliefs. Engaging in the participation of one or two such endeavors, or assuming the role of a volunteer for a charitable organization, can occupy your time adequately to alleviate the sensation of loneliness. Engaging with well-established organizations not only facilitates the cultivation of new companions, but also expedites the passage of time, thereby rendering the anticipation more tolerable.

Engage in additional employment.

If your main occupation does not entail excessive labor exceeding forty hours or encompassing five days per week, it is highly likely that a significant portion of your evenings and weekends is dedicated to leisure activities involving television and/or computer usage. Utilize your free time productively by pursuing employment opportunities during the weekends or evenings for three days a week.

Take up a hobby.

Have you consistently harbored an inclination towards acquiring skills in the field of oil-painting? What is the method of performing on a musical instrument? Grow tomatoes? Take classes, read books, join forums centered around your interest. Allocate dedicated time each day or week for immersing yourself in that particular hobby. It provides an excellent avenue for achieving personal satisfaction, particularly in cases where professional obligations might fall short, and serves as an effective outlet for alleviating stress. Additionally, it will help to maintain cognitive acuity as you advance in age.

Avoid baby/parenting books.

If your aspiration has always been to start a family, you may feel inclined to extensively peruse literature pertaining to pregnancy, infants, and childcare.

Resist the temptation. It possesses a comparable level of peril to partaking in the realm of dating. Indeed, it is imperative that you acquire ample knowledge regarding the requisites for fostering the well-being and contentment of children prior to embarking upon matrimony and commencing parenthood. Engaging in excessive pre-reading will lead to increased impatience, as one longs for the immediate presence of the fictional progenitor. It is possible that excessive reading could lead to a state of depression.

Don't do it.

Now, let us delve into one of the most contentious chapters in the book...

Give yourself a hand.

This chapter primarily focuses on the act of waiting as opposed to engaging in romantic relationships. However, in the event that, during the waiting period, one finds themselves ensnared in the grip of that particular monthly occurrence, resulting in a sensation of overwhelming heat. You may have experienced instances when, under certain circumstances, even individuals who are considered less appealing may appear more appealing or attractive to you. If one's hormonal activities are functioning optimally, such occurrences manifest on a monthly basis, lasting for a span of seven to ten days, with three to five of these days exhibiting a particularly heightened intensity.

Moreover, a significant factor prompting women to pursue relationships is their desire for sexual gratification. I intend to provide a comprehensive explanation of this matter in chapter seven, delving into intricate specifics. In the meantime, please permit me to highlight the concept that a woman can experience sexual gratification independently. I kindly request permission to discuss a topic that is typically avoided within religious circles: self-stimulation.

According to a published literature, it has been found that 97% of males engage in self-stimulation at some point in their lives, while the remaining 3% choose to withhold this information. Although the statement possesses a comedic undertone, it illuminates a significant omission: the acknowledgment that numerous women have never engaged in self-stimulation, and may lack the knowledge on how to initiate such an act, primarily due to society's historical discouragement of female masturbation throughout the ages. Numerous religious factions censure this action as a transgression, applicable to both sexes regardless of marital status; however, they tend to exhibit leniency towards their male adherents in regard to this conviction.

Perhaps due to the historically predominant representation of males in leadership positions within religious groups. Hmm.

Moving right along...

If you hold a firm conviction that masturbation is universally immoral and possess the personal discipline to abide by this belief, I encourage you to proceed accordingly. I genuinely mean it. You fail to comprehend the exceptional nature of your presence within contemporary society. Furthermore, there is no necessity to peruse any further sections of this chapter, as it is highly unlikely that you will engage in sexual relations with a gentleman prior to entering into the bonds of matrimony.

In my opinion, it is my firm belief that practicing self-control in relation to sexual gratification can be achieved by engaging in alternative activities such as taking a leisurely stroll, indulging in a refreshing cold shower, or seeking the company of others in a public setting at the earliest opportunity. Nevertheless, not all individuals will be able to attain the ideal, despite their efforts to do so. Under such circumstances, I would like to inquire: which option would be more advisable - to subject oneself to a recurrent cycle of emotional distress and potential consequences such as heartbreak and unintended pregnancy by engaging in sexual relationships with the men one dates, or to alleviate the sexual tension that arises approximately three to four days out of every thirty through self-stimulation?

I believe that the latter option would effectively safeguard you against numerous complications and distress. I would dare to assert that, in the context of unmarried individuals, the act of self-stimulation might not be deemed morally reprehensible.

To those who use the Bible as their life guidebook, I say this: the Bible is not totally clear on my previous statement, so you need to go to God yourself to get a straight answer. However, the Bible unequivocally states that within the context of matrimony, the responsibility to tend to one's spouse's needs in matters of sexual intimacy falls upon the husband. If you choose not to adhere to the principles outlined in the Bible and prefer to abstain from contemplating matters of morality, that is acceptable. However, I must introduce this aspect into the discourse for the betterment of my fellow believers.

There is, undoubtedly, a singular exception that applies solely to individuals who are not married. Any form of indulgence that develops into an addiction presents itself as a significant issue. If one finds oneself engaging in this activity on a daily basis, if social commitments have to be foregone in order to make time for it, if disciplinary issues arise at the workplace due to chronic lateness resulting from the necessity to satisfy this impulse before facing an unsavory superior – should any such circumstances manifest, it can be inferred that solitary sexual activity has progressed into an addictive behavior, necessitating professional intervention.

I posit that it is primarily due to this rationale that it has been vehemently discouraged. Certain individuals may encounter a significant issue with the aforementioned matter, similar to individuals who are incapable of consuming only one glass of wine per week without resorting to consuming ten glasses daily, or individuals who cannot partake in the Lottery once a month without depleting their retirement funds in Las Vegas. The experience of reaching climax could be considered an immensely compelling dependency, prompting me to exercise caution when contemplating the endorsement of the act of self-stimulation.

Develop self-awareness in this domain, and remain steadfast to your innate convictions. Please be aware that if your primary motivation for engaging in romantic relationships is solely to seek sexual gratification, there exists an alternative option that eliminates the need for contraceptive methods and mitigates the risk of contracting sexually transmitted infections.

***

Please take this opportunity to allocate a few moments to relax and recuperate from the mentally demanding content you have just encountered. Please hydrate yourself by consuming some water, engage in a brief stroll around the nearby vicinity, and indulge in the auditory pleasures of music.

Now we are approaching the enjoyable phase. Fortunately, for the majority of women, the period of waiting inevitably comes to a close, even if it occurs during their thirties, forties, or beyond.

How does one encounter an eligible gentleman in the absence of a romantic involvement, how does one discern a prospective life partner, and how does one establish acquaintance with said individual? It is considerably more convenient and secure compared to the approaches advocated by mainstream society.

In Light Of One's Reverence For Christ, It Is Incumbent Upon Individuals To Yield To One Another.

In accordance with the scripture from Genesis 2:21-25, it is narrated that the Divine Entity known as the LORD God induced a profound slumber to befall upon the male being, during which an instance of his rib was removed and subsequently sealed with tissue. And the rib that the LORD God had extracted from the man was fashioned into a woman, whom He then presented to the man. After these events unfolded, the male individual proclaimed, "Behold, this entity is of my own essence and physicality; henceforth she shall be identified as Woman, for she was derived from Man." Consequently, it is ordained that a male individual shall sever his ties with his paternal and maternal figures, and immerse himself completely in matrimony with his spouse, forming an indissoluble union and merging into a single entity. The man and his wife were both unclothed and felt no sense of embarrassment.

In accordance with Proverbs 18:22, the individual who discovers a life partner acquires that which is righteous and gains divine blessings.

Upon closer observation, one may notice the presence of certain absent ribs that require discovery in accordance with the principle of attraction. It is analogous to a magnetic force, wherein the act of finding those ribs becomes highly desired, particularly by women. Upon our initial encounter, it became unequivocally clear to me that my husband possessed all the qualities indicative of a destined soulmate. We have joyfully entered into matrimony and been blessed by the divine grace of God, resulting in the formation of a blissful union and the creation of a wonderful family comprising of three exceptional children.

Eph 5:21-32:

In light of our deep respect for Christ, let us mutually yield to one another.

Wives, submit to your husbands as to the Lord. The husband holds the position of authority over his wife, paralleling the way Christ leads and saves the church, which is his body. In accordance with the principles of the church, it is expected that wives demonstrate submission to their husbands in all matters, just as the church submits to Christ.

Spouses, express deep affection towards your life partners, in a manner akin to the way Christ demonstrated love for the church, sacrificing himself to sanctify and purify her. This purification is accomplished through the metaphorical act of washing with water, representing the transformative power of the word. The ultimate aim is to present the church to himself as a resplendent and untarnished entity, free from imperfections such as stains, wrinkles, or any other flaws, and in a state of complete holiness and innocence. Similarly, husbands are obliged to demonstrate affection towards their spouses, treating them with the same care and concern as they do towards their own physical well-being. The individual who possesses affection for their spouse demonstrates a reciprocal fondness towards their own person. In light of everything, it is worth noting that there exists no individual who harbors animosity towards their own physical being; rather, they nourish and attend to it, similar to the manner in which Christ tends to the church, as we, being part of His body, are intimately connected to Him.

Due to this premise, a man shall depart from his paternal and maternal figures and establish a bond with his spouse, resulting in their symbiotic integration as a singular entity.

This enigmatic occurrence persists; however, I am referring to the divine connection between Christ and the church.

We can acknowledge and value the intentions behind God's design for marriage, which include fostering companionship, nurturing spiritual closeness, and enabling joint devotion to God.

The notion of seeking a 'soulmate' to fulfill us, implying that another individual holds the key to our completion, poses a spiritual dilemma as it gravitates towards the act of idolatry. We are to find our fulfillment and purpose in God . If we place the expectation for our spouse to embody divine qualities, they will inevitably fall short on a daily basis. It is impracticable for an individual to meet such lofty expectations. Every individual experiences challenging days, engages in heated arguments with their partner, or exhibits moments of self-centeredness. Notwithstanding these flaws, it is the divine intention that the husband and wife serve as guiding forces for one another towards the path of the divine.

Whilst it is readily apparent why the Divine intended a union that prioritizes the needs and interests of others in a world characterized by self-centeredness, abiding by such a principle proves to be a formidable endeavor.

- The institution of marriage is divinely ordained, established as an enduring covenant between a male and a female.

Marriage represents the most solid cornerstone for establishing a family unit.

- Sexual expression is intended by a divine design to facilitate the development of intimacy between spouses.

Marriage serves as a reflection of God's sacred covenant with humanity.

This final correlation is evident throughout the entirety of the Bible. As an illustration, Jesus alludes to His own identity as the "bridegroom" and likens the realm of heaven to a "celebratory feast of matrimony."

These aforementioned points serve as evidence that the intentions of God regarding marriage extend beyond mere personal happiness. They emphasize that God does not oppose happiness itself, but rather, marriage serves to endorse loftier principles.

It is not within the divine intention for marriage to be solely established as a means to ensure the replenishment of the population and establish a stable societal structure for child-rearing. He introduced the institution of marriage among mankind as an additional indicator aiming towards His own everlasting, metaphysical existence.

If the pursuit of happiness is our ultimate objective, we may consider ending our marital union as soon as happiness appears to diminish. Similarly, should our foremost aspiration be to experience affection, we may contemplate severing ties with our spouse at the slightest indication of reduced attentiveness. However, if we enter into matrimony with the intention of honoring and glorifying God, exemplifying His love and dedication to our offspring, and manifesting His testament to humanity, the idea of divorce becomes illogical.

- Focus on your spouse's strengths rather than their weaknesses.

- Foster positive reinforcement rather than engage in criticism.

- Instead of engaging in gossipy conversations about your spouse, take a moment to offer prayers for them.

- Acquire and embody the teachings of Christ regarding interpersonal connections and compassion towards others.

This advice can be especially advantageous for young couples. Ultimately, quite a few couples embarking on the journey of marriage are ill-equipped to smoothly navigate the shift from sporadic encounters to the immediate cohabitation and complete sharing of their lives. It is highly likely that bothersome patterns of behavior and unattractive habits will become evident. However, as followers of the Christian faith, it is incumbent upon us to exhibit reverence towards all individuals, including our marital partner.

What Are Effective Strategies For Capturing The Affection And Commitment Of A Male Partner In A Romantic Relationship?

"He evoked a profound sense of disarray within me... As if he possessed the ability to dismantle my being and reconstruct it repeatedly." - Chelsie Shakespeare

When it pertains to persuading a gentleman to embrace a committed relationship, numerous women encounter difficulty in deciphering the enigma and unveiling the elusive technique of captivating a man's affections and instilling lasting desire, extending beyond the present moment and encompassing the anticipated entirety of a shared lifetime.

Given the propagation of myths such as "the key to capturing a man's affections lies in his stomach" (namely, one's culinary prowess), it is not entirely unexpected that we often fail to meet these expectations.

As witnessed by a majority of individuals, it can be generally observed that there exist two distinct categories of males in their romantic interactions with females.

Concealed behind the first curtain is an individual who is completely enthralled by his significant other. He holds her in high regard, bestows upon her the treatment befitting royalty, and prioritizes her happiness above his own.

The individual concealed behind curtain number two is commonly referred to as a commitment-phobic person. His demeanor suggests a lack of interest in engaging in romantic partnerships, giving the impression that any form of commitment he enters into is involuntary in nature.

However, despite the prevailing belief among most women that the second category of men is more common, statistical data reveals a different reality. According to the latest Singles In America report published by Match Group, it has been observed that a significant majority of Millennials, precisely 63 percent, express a desire to explore and cultivate passionate love. Furthermore, an impressive 70 percent of individuals belonging to Generation Z are motivated to seek a committed and enduring partnership. It is noteworthy that a mere 11 percent of Gen Z and Millennials engage in casual dating, reflecting a preference for more serious and purposeful romantic relationships.

Therefore, if the attainment of a profound and enduring romantic partnership is the prevailing aspiration amongst the majority, how does one successfully persuade their romantic partner to not only develop deep affection for them, but also cultivate a relentless longing that instigates a purposeful commitment?

Maintaining a man's long-term interest in staying with you ultimately revolves around his perception of commitment as a whole.

For many males, establishing a deep emotional connection can feel akin to solving a complex puzzle. If the elements needed for a successful bond are not aligned, he is more likely to maintain an emotional distance and unavailability rather than fully engaging. He was adept at formulating diverse concise rationales that women undoubtedly found exasperating, such as, "My main focus is on my professional pursuits," "I require personal solitude at the moment," or, "I am currently unprepared for a committed partnership."

It may come as a surprise, but these brief statements are not deceptive in nature. He holds the belief in his statements due to the fact that the numerical data that triggers his sense of dedication does not coincide with his desired alignment.

To rephrase in a more formal tone: To clarify, when an individual states, "Presently, I am not prepared for a romantic involvement," they are essentially conveying that they are not prepared to engage in a romantic relationship specifically with you.

Although this may cause discomfort upon hearing, understanding what is most likely to prompt them to eventually initiate commitment will help mitigate significant distress.

The fact of the matter is, once he encounters that particular woman who possesses the optimal sequence to unlock his commitment combination, he will feel compelled to remain in a relationship with her. He will willingly enter into a committed, enduring partnership, as he is averse to jeopardizing the potential loss of her presence.

Having established that commitment is not an aversion exclusive to males, your task now lies in unraveling the intricacies of deciphering his commitment code. Naturally, it is a challenge due to the common difficulty of men in effectively expressing their emotional needs, however, this is where these dating recommendations prove to be valuable.

Disclaimer: The process of capturing a man's affection is subjective and may vary depending on the individual; therefore, not all approaches will yield the same results for every man.

Outlined below are six effective approaches to capture a man's affection and establish an exclusive bond with him.

1. Illustrate to him the extent of your longing for him.

The strategy for capturing the affection of a resolute individual is likewise a hidden key to bringing joy into his life. It resonates with his intrinsic, primal longing.

Deep within his core, he must possess an intense longing for you, yearn for you, and yearn for your presence. It is imperative that he feel a sense of longing in your absence, and that he undergoes a surge of desire when a considerable period of time has elapsed since your last encounter.

This inclination is derived from the interplay of contrasting elements. He will develop a strong attraction towards you and then proceed to pursue you; he will experience longing for you and then gradually develop stronger feelings for you; he will eagerly seek your affection and then you will eventually submit to him. It entails the continuous generation and subsequent dissipation of tension.

The means by which you generate such tension lies in your allure, employing a subtle form of enticement followed by willing surrender, evoking a playful pursuit only to willingly succumb, infusing his life with elements of lightheartedness and impulsive ardor, casting lustful gazes and artfully departing the scene, discreetly sending provocative messages throughout the day, and embracing him unexpectedly with a passionate kiss.

How to achieve this objective: Seek out opportunities where you can adopt a more sensual, lighthearted, and alluring demeanor. Utilize your compelling feminine qualities to juxtapose his sincere and calculated masculine disposition. (Additional suggestion: Consider initiating intimate moments!)

2. Respect him.

Respect serves as an essential moral principle, serving as the bedrock for enduring connections that endure and withstand the trials of time. Exhibiting reverence can potentially revitalize a relationship well beyond the fading of affection and longing. Numerous men choose to wed the woman who displays a profound level of respect towards them, placing it above the affection expressed by another potential partner.

Men may engage in intimate relations, indulge in heartfelt conversations, and demonstrate genuine concern for the woman they deeply cherish (and covet), yet often, love alone does not fulfill all their emotional requirements. A considerable portion of this is attributed to the sentiment expressed in the phrase "I love you."

For both males and females, this expression may evoke different interpretations. An individual might interpret this as a plea to prevent harm or perhaps an assertion of confinement. Men tend to view affection from women as a mere transaction rather than as a novel experience.

Indeed, the expressions may bring about a sense of gratification upon reaching his ears, yet they fail to evoke a profound resonance within his inner being. Males possess significant vulnerabilities that they silently battle throughout their entire lifetimes.

Therefore, ascertain the reasons behind your admiration for the gentleman. For what reason do you take pride in his accomplishments? What merits can you attribute to him? What strategies can be employed to cultivate positive self-esteem in him? Then, tell him. It is advisable to not solely express your love for him, but instead provide explicit reasons for your affection.

An alternative method to demonstrate your regard is to express remorse following any errors or instances of uttering inappropriate remarks. It is imperative that both yourself and he prioritize the significance of the partnership over personal egos.

Once he comprehends the significance you place on his character, he will grant you deeper access, divulging additional vulnerable facets of his inner self that require healing and support.

Method of accomplishing this task: Seek approaches for acknowledging his efforts in areas that may otherwise be overlooked.

3. Establish a secure environment for his well-being.

It is imperative to consider the emotional well-being of a man while acquiring knowledge on how to capture his affection. It is imperative for him to experience a sense of emotional security. By releasing your wrath, hate, or any animosity you feel against him, you offer him safe access to be vulnerable. He experiences a sense of liberation in expressing his true self when he is in your presence.

This phenomenon transpires when you place your trust in him by making investments. Subsequently, he will develop a sense of trust towards you. Both of you demonstrate a willingness to embrace vulnerability, which is a crucial factor in achieving a successful relationship. However, in order for this vulnerability to gain momentum, it is frequently necessary for women to take the lead. Males are in search of an individual who can guide them through the depths of vulnerability.

A woman exhibits the courage to be vulnerable, thereby eliciting a response from men to lower their emotional defenses and experience a sense of ease.

Could you please explain the procedure for accomplishing this task? It is advantageous to acquire an understanding of the male thought process. It is important for him to be aware that you will refrain from passing judgment or offering criticism. It is important to provide him with a sense of support, acceptance, and encouragement, demonstrating that you are actively aligned with him. He must be made aware of the fact that you will maintain utmost confidentiality by refraining from sharing any missteps committed by him with your acquaintances, especially your mother.

It is imperative for him to be aware that you will support him in the face of derogatory remarks made about him. He desires to ascertain your commitment to confronting any instances of injustice or adversity directly.

Approaching this objective entails placing confidence in oneself and recognizing one's capacity to exhibit vulnerability in his presence, for this mutual unveiling allows the establishment of an authentic connection between the two individuals.

4. Challenge him.

Every individual is inherently faced with a challenge at their core. Men develop through difficulty. The challenge evokes a deep sense of masculine drive that compels them to seek victory and triumph. The pursuit of challenge is the path that individuals undertake in order to achieve their goals, thereby leading to a sense of recognition and gratification.

In essence, it ultimately comes down to possessing a robust understanding of your principles – acknowledging what holds utmost significance to you and steadfastly adhering to it. This presents a dilemma that enhances the bond.

One additional factor of this daunting task entails confronting an individual when one perceives a compromise of these very principles. It may be necessary for you to address this matter directly with him if you believe he owes you an apology, instead of allowing it to be disregarded.

Upon the occasion that you are able to confront him directly, he shall perceive your countenance as significantly captivating. Although he may initially respond with anger, your ability to assert yourself will ultimately alter his perception of you. It will serve as an impetus for his personal growth and development as an individual.

5. Embrace your femininity.

The next step in winning a man is just old-fashioned excitement. It is critical for him to experience profound admiration and astonishment when contemplating your presence. Engaging in slightly eccentric behavior can be positive, but it is important to draw a distinction between eccentricity and irrationality. For instance, taking a spontaneous swim in the ocean may be considered favorable, whereas feigning a kidnapping incident due to one's partner working late hours is not.

Regrettably, there is a pervasive tendency to instruct women to experience negative emotions regarding their emotional nature, to perceive themselves as irrational, and to view their behavior as erratic. However, men are often drawn to these feminine attributes, so do not hesitate to embrace your unconventional side.

Embrace and cultivate your innate femininity, allowing it to invigorate and enhance your relationship. This may contribute to intensifying a gentleman's romantic feelings towards you. By embracing your innate feminine essence, you create an environment where he feels compelled to express his admiration for you, remarking, "There is an inexplicable charm about her that captivates me."

How to achieve this objective: Embrace your true identity and fulfill your intended purpose.

6. Promote and facilitate his objective.

Similar to hindrances, exceptional individuals must possess a sense of purpose in life. Individuals of the male gender necessitate a sense of direction and meaning in their existence, whether it entails striving to become an exemplary life partner or attaining the highest stature within their professional domain.

Support his work ethic. Foster his re-engagement in hobbies he abandoned, or help him discover latent passions he may possess.

To garner his affection, demonstrate resilience by confronting individuals who belittle him or endeavor to undermine his sense of value. Commend his exceptional capacity for wholehearted support and encouragement towards others. To gain favor with a man, it is important to support and encourage his heartfelt desires.

How to achieve this: Express genuine admiration and appreciation for his accomplishments and qualities.

There is no necessity for one to adopt a masculine mindset in order to achieve success in interpersonal relationships with men, nor is it essential to suppress one's inherent femininity in order to establish and maintain a functional connection. Express yourself freely, embrace your inner wildness, unleash your theatrical persona, and delight in the joyous experience. Own it. He will hold a greater affection for you as a result.

Ensure That You Maintain Your Profile.

Given the scale of the Internet, it is possible that one may encounter difficulty in navigating the vastness of cyberspace while seeking an ideal romantic partner. If one engages in online dating, they are undoubtedly seeking a partner of upstanding character and unwavering devotion. It is reasonable to anticipate the presence of numerous individuals with inappropriate or untrustworthy intentions, or even individuals possessing attractive physical features, but lacking depth of character. Thus, what measures do you undertake to ensure you encounter an ideal partner?

To effectively appeal to a suitable and discerning gentleman, it is advisable to ensure that your profile possesses the qualities that would capture the attention of such individuals. Please bear in mind that your profile serves as your identification within the realm of online dating. This is the initial impression perceived by a potential date, preceding any other observations. If you desire to captivate the attention of individuals belonging to your specific type, it is imperative to construct a profile that effectively exemplifies your finest qualities. Ensure to bear in mind the subsequent suggestions, and you will undoubtedly capture the attention of individuals belonging to your specific category.

Men are visual

Given that males tend to be visually oriented, their initial focus will typically be directed towards your facial features. Ensure that your profile picture exhibits a joyful countenance. Individuals of the male gender demonstrate an inherent inclination towards visual stimuli featuring representations of females displaying a positive facial expression, specifically smiles. Ensure that your photograph is current as well. This will project an image of a positive, energetic, and engaging individual, characteristics highly sought after by their preferences.

Exhibit ingenuity in responding to inquiries.

When responding to inquiries on dating platforms, it is imperative to construct narratives that vividly depict scenarios, enabling men to envision themselves actively participating. Strive to present yourself in an engaging manner while maintaining authenticity. For instance, in the event that you are being queried pertaining to your notion of an exceptional rendezvous, ensure that you incorporate enjoyable elements, while also ensuring your genuine affinity towards the activities mentioned. Incorporate vivid vocabulary into your statements. Construct a roster detailing the activities you desire to engage in, such as picnicking, while ensuring the incorporation of his presence through the use of inclusive pronouns such as "we."

Minimize the I's

In the realm of digital interactions, one must adeptly seize the attention of a gentleman within a limited span of ten seconds. Should he grow weary of excessive self-references, he will swiftly redirect his attention elsewhere. It is advisable to reduce instances of self-mention and ensure that one's statements are consistently engaging. Upon contemplation, it becomes apparent that encountering individuals at social gatherings who solely engage in discussions pertaining to their personal interests and repeatedly express their preferences possess a propensity to generate a tedious atmosphere.

Ensure that your profiles possess an engaging quality.

Interests and hobbies play a significant role in fostering social cohesion, as they have the ability to bring individuals closer in connection. Particularly with regard to individuals who have an affinity for sports, this is likely to pique the interest of men. Conversely, in the initial phase of acquaintance, it is not requisite for gentlemen to possess comprehensive knowledge regarding your personal details. Please refrain from disclosing additional personal information until the occasion of your inaugural rendezvous. That would present an opportune moment for the both of you to engage in the exchange of compelling and significant anecdotes. Ultimately, the objective of creating a profile is to attract the attention and interest of a respectable individual, prompting them to desire a rendezvous with you.

Leave Your Emotional Baggage

If you continue to struggle with moving on from a past relationship, it is possible that you have not reached a state of readiness to pursue a new romantic connection. In the realm of online dating, it is advisable to convey a favorable and optimistic demeanor within your profile, as well as in your written exchanges. Prior to embarking on a quest for a prospective companion, it is essential to consign your past experiences to history and refrain from allowing them to impede your present endeavors.

Conclude your profile by posing a compelling inquiry

Consider concluding your profile by kindly inviting gentlemen who are captivated by your profile to initiate communication with you. As an illustration, it is possible to inquire about their preferences or ascertain whether they share an interest in your pursuits.

Don't Make Demands

Please refrain from discussing remuneration and expressing preferences for fine dining establishments in your locality. Even individuals of substantial wealth would be unlikely to pursue relationships with women who assert control over their choices and preferences. In the majority of instances, it is observed that men have already encountered a sufficient number of demands and responsibilities throughout their lives, therefore, they are not actively seeking the addition of unfamiliar obligations from others.

Remain authentic to your true self.

Do not engage in the act of feigning an identity that deviates from your true self. Maintain genuine authenticity at all times. Alternatively, if not, it would amount to misleading promotional practices. Maintaining the facade of a specific persona in an attempt to allure a "high-caliber" man would prove immensely challenging. Please bear in mind that you do not possess control over the personal preferences or aspirations of a gentleman, however, you do possess the ability to determine your own criteria for a high-caliber partner.

Don't Focus On One

It is essential to adopt a prudent approach when pursuing romantic relationships. Placing excessive reliance on a single individual, rather than maintaining a diverse dating experience, can ultimately lead to disillusionment in the event of an unfavorable outcome. Ensure that you maintain a mindset of flexibility and actively appreciate the admiration you receive from multiple suitors, rather than exclusively fixating on immediately identifying your ideal partner The suitable individual will eventually appear during your pursuit, but in the meantime, there are numerous enjoyable experiences you can have with a temporary companion.

Make an effort to dedicate a portion of your time to the act of writing.

Make a commitment to yourself to diligently craft a profile that exudes a subtle charm and captivates the attention of potential online suitors. Ensure it strikes the perfect balance between being alluring and compelling, while still being concise and engaging. It is comprehensible that you may lose motivation in completing a comprehensive profile detailing your personal information once you have established your account. Nevertheless, it is important to consider that when a gentleman exhibits interest in your photograph, he will assuredly peruse your About Me section in order to glean additional information about your persona. There have been instances where attractive women were not contacted due to the absence of any content in their biography section. The biography holds the secondary importance for male individuals while viewing your profile. This aids in their decision-making process regarding whether to engage in conversation with you. Utilize your biography to elucidate your attributes, pastimes, and the valuable contributions you bring in the context of interpersonal connections. Furthermore, it is imperative to consistently include a delightful photograph showcasing a warm smile, as this will undoubtedly create an ideal impression capable of capturing the attention of your desired gentleman.

Find Your Dream Man!

Having identified your priorities and desires in a relationship, it is now time for you to excel in the realm of dating. Your profile will serve as a discerning mechanism, ensuring the exclusion of individuals who do not meet your criteria, while simultaneously attracting men seeking someone with your qualities. It is important to bear in mind that individuals may not possess the same level of preparedness as you do when venturing into the realm of online dating. Therefore, it is advisable to exercise patience and invest sufficient time in acquainting yourself with the individual before reaching a decision regarding the feasibility of an in-person meeting. In order to optimize the effectiveness of your profile, it is essential to consistently consider both your personal identity and your objectives. Do not allow yourself to become diverted solely by attractive countenances or captivating personal narratives. Ensure that prior to initiating a conversation with someone, ascertain that they possess the appearance that aligns with your criteria. The foremost principle of the dating sphere is to remain authentic, as the ultimate objective of dating is to discover a life partner with whom one can share a lifetime. The endeavor to locate him might require a considerable amount of time, but by exercising patience, you shall eventually encounter an exemplary gentleman.

Discerning Your Desired Object Of Interest

After establishing a strong sense of personal confidence, you are prepared to initiate your search. May I inquire about the specific objective you are seeking to achieve? Before you get carried away, let's not sit down and start making lists of every single thing that would make a person "perfect." The important thing to remember is that you aren't creating your perception of a perfect mate — you're looking for another real person.

It is imperative to take note of the outward characteristics that you seek as the initial step. Each individual possesses their own set of physical preferences, and while these preferences are acceptable, it is worth contemplating if they contribute positively to your overall well-being. Naturally, you do not wish to relinquish them entirely. If an individual identifies as gay, it is unlikely that their romantic or attractional interests would shift towards individuals of the opposite gender. Similarly, if one does not experience attraction towards older individuals, it would be improbable for them to consider pursuing a romantic relationship with someone who is twice their age. Nevertheless, it might be advisable not to firmly uphold alternative inclinations. Instances of this phenomenon may include characteristics such as precise stature, complexion, eye pigmentation, or hair pigmentation. By stating, "My preference lies solely in dating individuals with blonde hair," you are significantly excluding a considerable portion of the general populace who could potentially be your ideal life partner.

Instead of assigning significance to trivial and superficial characteristics, compile a collection of qualities that you desire in your ideal life partner. Begin with those that hold the highest priority and proceed in descending order. One may argue that documenting certain attributes, such as kindness, may appear superfluous. However, if it holds significance for you, it is advisable to incorporate it in your account. Please proceed with the examination of social, political, and religious factors as they pertain to the subject matter. If it is of utmost importance that you pursue a romantic relationship with another individual who shares the Jewish faith, or that your ideal partner aligns with a moderate political stance, please include it in your considerations. The longstanding proverb advising against discussing religion or politics on initial

dates ought to be set aside. Discovering, half a year into a romantic bond, that there exists an irreconcilable difference, which one or both parties consider as non-negotiable, would be an unfortunate circumstance to encounter.
Nevertheless, it is important to acknowledge that certain couples have formed the foundation of their relationship based on their lack of awareness regarding a significant factor that may have appeared crucial initially. Once they had developed romantic feelings for each other, that specific truth ceased to serve as a legitimate impediment to their relationship.

Lastly, take into consideration the qualities that you believe would contribute to the pleasurable nature of a relationship. These can be described by adjectives such as impromptu, enduring, tranquil, or humorous.

In this manner, as you commence actively seeking for the ideal life partner, you will possess the knowledge of which inquiries to pose. This assists in acquainting oneself with the individual and delving deeper into their character, thereby surpassing the frequently superficial questionnaires featured on dating platforms.

Chapter Two

This guided meditation aims to cultivate your consciousness towards the manifestation of your ideal life partner through a focus on the desired qualities. Please review your written list prior to commencing. Begin:

Please take a seat and make yourself comfortable.

If one is seated on the floor, it is advisable to employ a pillow or cushion in order to ensure that the hips are elevated above the knees.

When you are seated, ensure that your feet are positioned firmly on the floor.

Maintain an upright posture and refrain from crossing your legs. This facilitates enhanced oxygenation and fosters heightened relaxation.

Inhale deeply and rhythmically, allowing the breath to originate from the diaphragm. Hold. And release.

Gently shut your eyes and sense as the unease, uncertainty, and apprehension within your body gradually diminishes, gradually shifting towards your essence and permeating into your lungs.

With every inhalation, perceive the radiant intensification of your inner being akin to a guiding light.

With every exhalation, experience the departure of tension, doubt, and anxiety from your being, creating an empty void.

As you inhale, experience the sensations of warmth, affection, solace, and assurance emanating from every breath, permeating the void within you. Relaxing you, calming you.

Relax your shoulders while gradually breathing out any feelings of tension, uncertainty, and unease, and inhaling a sense of warmth, affection, tranquility, and reassurance.

Experience the virtues that you desire in your life partner as their energies gracefully envelop your essence. Intense and Vibrant.

As you inhale the qualities of warmth, love, comfort, and security, draw in these attributes as well. They approach you with a genuine willingness.

Maintain consistent diaphragmatic breathing, releasing any tension, uncertainty, or unease, while inhaling the positive qualities, affection, solace, and assurance emanating from your soul mate.

As you maintain a steady respiration, delve into the recesses of your consciousness and recollect an instance in your existence wherein you harbored profound and authentic affection towards an individual within your sphere. Recognize the moment when an individual conveyed an intense and genuine affection for you. Make an effort to fully comprehend every aspect of this moment. In which location did this occurrence transpire? At what time? Can you smell anything? How did you feel?

With each inhalation, fully embrace this memory, allowing it to flourish in vividness, while permitting this sentiment to permeate within you, escalating in brilliance with every breath taken in.

Preserve these emotions while permitting the recollection to diminish.

Please be mindful of your emotional state while maintaining an objective perspective. Please take into consideration whether your heart feels invigorated or melancholic. Does it lack weight or is it heavily laden? Does your heart possess a sense of warmth, or does it exude a sense of coldness, or perhaps it remains in a state of tepidity?

While you retain these emotions, request to establish a connection with your destined life partner.

Refrain from hastening as you permit yourself to immerse in the energy of your destined companion. It will occur at its own pace.

Please proceed with sustained deep breaths, allowing yourself to receive additional energy from your compatible soul companion.

Retain these emotions as every inhalation guides you towards your essence, towards the depths of your innermost being. In the space there. During the profound and intertwining bond with your soul mate.

Upon concluding your meditation session, it is advisable to retain these emotions and recollect the sentiments evoked within your heart during the practice. It has the potential to evolve in accordance with your shifting preferences and aspirations.

Before your date

If the individual in question is someone whom you have encountered on the internet, it would be prudent to engage in some investigative measures to ascertain his authenticity. Conduct exhaustive online research to acquaint yourself with his background, ascertain his age, profession, and any additional information in order to ensure your peace of mind.

If you share common acquaintances, you may consider soliciting insights from individuals familiar with him and urging them to share any pertinent information for your discretion.

Please kindly confirm your availability for a mutually suitable date and time to hold a meeting. In the event that you are aware of your long working hours throughout the entire week and proceed to schedule a social engagement on

Friday night when you are fatigued, it is highly unlikely that you will be able to present yourself in the most optimal manner.

Please refrain from engaging in excessive alcohol consumption or socializing the night before your scheduled rendezvous. Despite your sense of excitement, your physical appearance may appear fatigued.

Ensure that you are adequately rejuvenated and in a state of calm. In the event that you experienced a day filled with great stress prior to the planned engagement, it would be advisable to allocate a portion of your time for engaging in activities such as meditation, embarking on a serene stroll, or adhering to a personal ritual that aims to alleviate your anxieties.

Please cleanse yourself and groom your hair. Commence your preparations with ample time to avoid being delayed and hurriedly completing your tasks.

Determine the nature of the location you are about to visit. The choice of attire will vary depending on the setting, with a distinguishable disparity between what is appropriate for a high-end establishment and what is suitable for a casual outdoor excursion.

Irrespective of the kind of attire one chooses, it is imperative that it is maintained in a pristine condition while also embodying a sense of style.

Ensure that you organize your living area and thoroughly clean your vehicle in the event that there is a likelihood of him encountering them.

Please consider formulating some open-ended inquiries to pose to him in the event of a lull in the dialogue.

My perspective on attending a cinema screening for an initial rendezvous

Attending a movie or concert as a first date activity, without any subsequent plans, is deemed unfavorable. During the course of a film, it is not possible to engage in mutual communication or establish personal connections. Nevertheless, engaging in a post-movie dining experience serves the purpose of providing a topic of discussion in the event that you encounter challenges in initiating conversation. The rationale for not considering dinner prior to the movie stems from the potential for an unpleasant experience, which could subsequently detract from one's overall enjoyment of the film.

An improved concept for a initial rendezvous

If you have yet to have a face-to-face encounter, it is advisable to choose a location that allows for a swift and uncomplicated departure, should the need arise. A coffee establishment is secure and straightforward. If you have prior acquaintance with the individual and aim to leave a positive impact, you can elevate the encounter by arranging a meeting over drinks or a meal. Alternatively, engaging in physical activities such as taking a stroll or participating in a recreational sport can be considered. Arrange to convene at a mutually convenient public location.

During your date

Were you aware that during the initial stages of getting acquainted with a prospective romantic partner, their perception of you is predominantly influenced by 55% due to your physical appearance and nonverbal cues, 38% attributed to your manner of speaking, and a mere 7% concerning the content of your actual words? Hence, the significance of presenting oneself in an impeccable manner cannot be underestimated. If you possess an attraction towards him, your non-verbal cues will undoubtedly manifest such sentiments, which has the potential to captivate his attention towards you as well. One's manner of speech serves as a reflection of their personality, and the presence of genuine enthusiasm will be evident in their vocal expression.

Have a positive attitude. The purpose of the occasion is to derive pleasure, therefore, it is advisable to display frequent smiles and actively engage in acquainting oneself with a novel individual.

Make eye contact. It is possible to engage in flirtation through the act of gazing into one another's eyes. It is a nuanced and profound method of fostering a connection without verbal communication.

Keep the conversation light. It is not necessary to solely engage in discussions pertaining to surface-level matters, yet it is advisable to refrain from delving into weighty subjects during the initial rendezvous.

Please refrain from interrupting him while he is speaking. Pay careful attention and demonstrate genuine interest in his discourse, incorporating insightful inquiries if desired.

When engaging in verbal communication, it is important to maintain a positive and cheerful tone in your voice. It is imperative to maintain an energetic demeanour and refrain from exhibiting any traces of negativity when engaging in verbal communication.

Strive to achieve a harmonious equilibrium between speaking and listening. The objective of the encounter is to present and exchange our individual characters, with the aim of determining our suitability and compatibility.

Be yourself. If one conceals their true self during an initial encounter, the need to continue feigning shall persist throughout the entirety of the ensuing relationship.

Inject a touch of levity into the discourse. Utilizing humor can effectively alleviate tension and generate a more relaxed atmosphere, especially in instances where one may feel anxious or have exhausted conversational subjects.

Stay present. Should you engage in the exhaustive scrutiny of his actions and words, you risk overlooking the essence of his message. You may engage in analysis at your convenience in solitude.

Be friendly and polite. Both parties involved are assuming some level of risk as they evaluate their compatibility and determine whether they wish to continue pursuing a romantic relationship. Thus, there is no necessity for one to display discourtesy.

Making conversation

If you truly harbor genuine affection for the individual with whom you are on a date, there is a possibility that you might experience the inclination to incessantly converse about your personal experiences and lavishly extol the virtues of your enchanting existence. Alternatively, at the opposite end of the continuum, you could pose numerous inquiries with the sole purpose of acquiring knowledge solely about his individuality. Both of these approaches are unsatisfactory. It is advisable to allow the conversation to unfold naturally. There ought to be a reciprocal exchange of information during the course of the rendezvous, whereby one party discloses a personal detail, followed by the other participant reciprocating with an equally significant contribution.

If one were to solely engage in self-centered conversation, it is likely that one's companion would become disinterested and vexed, perceiving a lack of consideration towards the latter's own experiences and interests. Alternatively, conversely, in contrast, seeking an abundance of information could potentially resemble a professional interview in his perspective. It is permissible to inquire, however, endeavor to limit your queries to those that are open-ended in nature (inquiries that necessitate more than a simple yes or no answer or a specific factual detail).

Please ensure you give your utmost attention to your companion during the designated time. In the event that his eyes exhibit signs of disinterest, it would be appropriate to divert the conversation towards a different topic or pose a thought-provoking inquiry to capture his attention.

Please demonstrate kindness and respect towards all individuals, not exclusively towards your companion. He will observe your interactions with waitstaff and unfamiliar individuals. Refrain from expressing discontent or dissatisfaction, and maintain a receptive mindset throughout the duration of the encounter.

May I inquire about the possibility of a farewell kiss?

If you experienced a strong connection with your companion, concluding your date with a brief and affectionate farewell kiss could serve as a splendid conclusion. There are individuals who hold the belief that it is inappropriate to engage in kissing during an initial encounter, and I hold a considerable level of admiration for their perspective. Should the individual make an unsolicited attempt at kissing, one may opt to turn their head, causing the gesture to land on their cheek, or to bypass the intended lips altogether and substitute it with a hug.

After your date

The primary step you ought to take is to introspect upon your sentiments pertaining to the rendezvous. It may be apparent that you experienced a strong connection or no connection at all. Alternatively, you may have doubts or uncertainty, hence the significance of this particular step.

Please endeavor to address and assess your emotions within the next 24-hour period. Do you experience a sense of joy and happiness whenever thoughts of him cross your mind? Alternatively, do you experience physical discomfort and recoil at the mere idea of encountering him once more? If you remain uncertain, refrain from immediately dismissing him. In order to arrive at a decision, it may be necessary for you to cultivate a more profound understanding of his character and qualities.

Now, you have the opportunity to scrutinize all of his behaviors and remarks. Has he made any notable remarks or actions that left a lasting impression on you? Do any warning signs or cause for concern arise? In the event that he made a remark that unsettled you, yet it does not constitute a decisive factor, would you be inclined to allow him an opportunity to offer a defense and clarify his rationale behind uttering such words?

While it may be enticing to initiate contact with him beforehand, refrain from doing so. Whilst you proceed with your post-date activities, he adheres to his own established routine that he must adhere to at his preferred pace. Although you may have taken the initiative to ask him out, it is essential that he assumes the role of an assertive individual and actively pursues you going forward. If he fails to extend another invitation, it may be indicative of a lack of interest on his part.

Regardless of who made the first move, it is customary for the man to take the initiative for the second date. I have erred in the practice of requesting the company of gentlemen not only for initial engagements, but also for subsequent occasions, including second, third, fourth, and beyond. One issue associated with this is the alteration of the balance between males and females. I adhere to feminist principles and advocate for women empowering themselves by assertively pursuing their desires. Nevertheless, when it comes to the realm of romantic relationships, assuming the lead role tends to convey a message to the male counterpart to assume a passive position and exhibit a lack of initiative. He will anticipate me to assume responsibility in devising all the arrangements and persist in courting him. He will not be able to regain that power, and it is highly likely that he will experience disinterest in the relationship, leading him to eventually depart.

If you exhibit a tendency to exert control in relationships and possess a preference for assuming leadership roles, then transitioning into equitable planning partners following a handful of dates could represent a highly beneficial middle ground. It is advisable to grant the gentleman the opportunity to court you, as this will allow him to experience a sense of masculinity, while simultaneously unveiling your own qualities as a leader.

Regrettably, if you had found the initial date to be delightful but have not received any further communication from him, it would be advisable to release any lingering attachments. He's not for you.

In the event that he reaches out to you and you are unequivocally disinterested, it is advisable not to prolong the interaction unnecessarily. Give a gentle rejection. Disregarding his advances following his invitation is simply unkind. I refrain from accepting an invitation for a second date from a gentleman only in instances where he chooses to initiate contact after a lapse of one month. It invokes speculation within me whether he engaged in social interactions with multiple other individuals of the opposite sex during that period, subsequently concluding that he would establish a committed relationship with me.

There are individuals who may prefer a lack of response, but personally, I believe in transparent and truthful communication. I have received a diverse range of unfavorable responses upon expressing the fact that we are not compatible. These reactions have encompassed instances where individuals have resorted to yelling, abruptly ending the conversation, enumerating my perceived negative qualities, and even making inappropriate assumptions about my sexual orientation. If for no other reason, it bolsters my confidence in my resolve to never encounter them again.

In the event that he initiates communication regarding a subsequent meeting and you hold an inclination towards him, you are progressing positively towards achieving a successful outcome. However, if you remain uncertain about your sentiments towards him, I would advise consenting to another rendezvous in order to gain further clarity.

A night of firsts...

At the age of fifteen, I dedicated all my leisure hours over the past few weeks conversing with Will, an individual I had encountered at a social gathering. I possessed a significant infatuation for him and eagerly anticipated the prospect of embarking on a formal outing, which would mark my inaugural rendezvous of such nature. The approaching event of Purim, a Jewish holiday, entails a joyous congregation characterized by participants adorning costumes and commemorating the deliverance of the Jewish community. Due to my continuous discussions about Will, my parents have permitted me to extend an invitation to him for our synagogue, despite him not being of Jewish faith.

My mother collected Will during our travel, and my father convened with us at the synagogue to partake in the commemoration. I greatly enjoyed the opportunity to be seated next to Will and partake in the festivities alongside someone who lacked familiarity with the Jewish faith. Throughout the entire night, I experienced a pervasive tingling sensation in my entire body. Despite my lack of comprehension regarding the term "sexual tension," it accurately describes the sensation I was experiencing.

Will must have sensed it as well, for the moment we returned to my mother's vehicle and settled in, he initiated gentle contact by caressing my leg. That swiftly transitioned to his hands ascending my physique and caressing my chest. It wasn't particularly enjoyable due to the presence of a fabric barrier, yet it marked my initial encounter with a gentleman touching my chest, or engaging in any kind of physical contact, for that matter.

It was evident to me that Will was determined to maximize our brief car journey and thus, he refrained from any unnecessary delays. Shortly after initiating contact with my bosom, he proceeded to draw closer and plant a kiss upon my person. That was my initial experience of kissing, however, his actions extended beyond that. He maintained continual contact with my lips over the course of fifteen minutes, simultaneously sliding his hands beneath my shirt, ensuring direct contact with my skin.

I was completely absorbed in our passionate exchange that the presence of the outside world dissipated. I am uncertain if I derived particular enjoyment from it; however, it was undeniably exhilarating to engage in my inaugural intimate encounter with an individual of the male gender for whom I held strong affection. I perceived the sound of a vehicle's horn resonating from a distant location, which swiftly jolted me back to my present state of consciousness. I briefly cast a glance towards my mother and noticed her radiant gaze fixed upon me via the reflection in the rearview mirror. I was taken aback and silently reflected upon the situation. My mother has recently borne witness to my inaugural experience of sharing a kiss with another individual. And the inaugural occurrence of my intimate encounter. And the initial instance when a gentleman made physical contact with my chest.

Will detected a momentary cessation in our intimate embrace, prompting him to approach my mother and request permission to join me in the sanctuary of my quarters for a few hours. My mother firmly asserted, 'No!'" Will attempted to kiss me once more, however, I recoiled and deftly brushed his hands aside from my person. We escorted him and experienced a quiet journey back to our residence. I experienced immense euphoria upon experiencing my inaugural kiss, yet I was simultaneously perturbed upon discovering the presence of my mother as an observer. In addition to my prevailing discomfort, my mother approached me later that evening and engaged in a discussion popularly referred to as "the talk."

Will contacted me the following day to initiate a discussion pertaining to our initial outing. We reached a consensus that the experience was remarkable, however, my prevailing sense of embarrassment overshadowed my enthusiasm for that particular evening. We engaged in a few additional conversations over the phone, yet each time I recollected Will, my thoughts were invariably accompanied by the disapproving gaze of my mother.

My conclusion: I undeniably experienced an evening of noteworthy initial experiences. I experienced the initial outing with a romantic interest, the inaugural sharing of a kiss, the initial encounter of intimate contact with a male, and engaging in the challenging conversation regarding human sexuality with my mother. I did not engage in subsequent encounters with Will, yet I derived some solace from the fact that I encountered, for the first time, a gentleman whose affection was reciprocated towards me.

What Is The Path To Reconnecting With One's Authentic Self?

If one finds oneself disconnected from their authentic self, what steps can be taken to align with the divine blueprint for their existence? It is imperative for you to modify certain behaviors while concurrently fostering novel patterns of behavior.

For Women

If you identify as a woman with a feminine disposition, I am confident that you have observed the distinct contrast in your emotional state when you are attired in elegant garments compared to more casual attire. Do you not experience an improved sense of self-worth? It is highly probable that you have also observed the awareness of others towards you, leading them to potentially alter their behavior in response. As per Shania Twain's assertion, one must experience the sensation of being in the state of feeling like a woman. There exist a multitude of methods to assist in enhancing one's feminine traits. "Presented below is a compilation of several resources that may be of assistance:

paint your nails

Please ensure that you are wearing pink or provocative undergarments beneath your professional attire.

Adorn garments that evoke a sense of well-being

Ensure that you groom your hair and apply makeup skillfully.

Initiate the playing of musical tunes and engage in rhythmic movements.

appreciate you

Women exhibit strength and authority when they embrace their feminine essence. Rest assured, I am well aware of the heightened comfort provided by sweatpants as compared to more stylish alternatives, albeit carrying a distinct difference in one's perception. A significant proportion of women exhibit pronounced self-criticism, a sentiment that is deeply disheartening. I too, can count myself among those women.

If one finds themselves in a state of poor physical fitness and harboring dissatisfaction towards their appearance, it becomes imperative to pledge a commitment to oneself regarding the initiation of exercising regularly and adopting a more nutritious dietary regimen. Upon commencing physical exercise, the initial instances may present challenges; nevertheless, subsequent repetitions shall become increasingly manageable. The additional you engage in physical exercise, the greater your likelihood of self-reflection in front of a mirror. You will begin to observe discernible transformations in your physique, alongside an enhanced sense of physical power and flexibility. Engaging in activities such as walking up the stairs can effectively improve your physical well-being. You will experience a heightened awareness of your body's musculature, prompting a desire for further indulgence. It will truly begin to evoke a profound sense of gratification.

Reflect upon this matter with utmost sincerity: if one finds difficulty in meeting their own gaze in the mirror while attired, and especially unclothed, it is imperative to consider the detrimental impact this would have on interpersonal connections. A gentleman whom you encounter shall kindly bestow upon you a compliment, yet you promptly refute it due to personal dissension. That would likely greatly diminish his interest. Do you do this? An individual desires a female companion who possesses self-love and self-respect, and is able to express gratitude gracefully upon receiving a compliment. You strive to embody the type of woman who elicits a profound sense of admiration from men, irrespective of physique. They are attracted to women of that nature. Queen Latifah has never exhibited a diminutive physique, yet her unparalleled self-assurance, inherent femininity, and exquisite physical features are truly remarkable.

Women, regardless of their physical attributes, are defined by their self-possession and demeanor. Every individual possesses imperfections;

however, it is important to embrace and cherish these imperfections. Love everything about you. It constitutes your unique identity. If your innate essence embodies femininity, engage in activities that evoke such sentiments. It bestows an unparalleled sense of liberation. I have observed women undergo a transition from exuding masculine qualities to embodying feminine attributes within a brief span of time, particularly at various Tony Robbins events. As a result, there is a noticeable transformation in their aura and physical presentation. It is quite captivating.

For Men
If you are an individual who identifies as a masculine male, yet find yourself deviating from behaviors and practices aligned with this identity, it is imperative to reintegrate activities and pursuits that evoke a sense of masculinity within you. During the Date With Destiny seminar, under the

guidance of Tony Robbins, attendees are informed that on a specific day of the event, there will be an absence of unoccupied seats in the venue due to the emotionally compelling nature of the program. While it may be considered lacking refinement, it is the occasion on which Tony encourages individuals to embody their respective masculine or feminine attributes. The females engage in the activity while the males observe, and subsequently, the males partake in the activity while the females observe.

He persuades the individuals to recall the pivotal moment preceding the climactic battle sequence in the film Braveheart, wherein William Wallace delivers an impassioned discourse aimed at motivating the soldiers to combat for their liberation. He skillfully projects the scene onto the grandiose cinema screen and successfully convinces all male attendees to exclaim in unison, 'FREEDOM! FREEDOM! FREEDOM!' The resounding chorus of more than a thousand fervent male voices renders an electrifying ambiance in the room, creating great exhilaration among the female spectators.

When one exudes confidence and a sense of invincibility, it becomes apparent to others, particularly women. I am not suggesting that it is necessary for every male to possess a muscular physique or engage in crude behavior in order to embody masculinity. Rather, I am emphasizing the importance of a man projecting a sense of self-assurance and having a strong presence.

To get a feminine woman, she needs to feel your presence. It is imperative that she has the perception that you will provide her with proper care. This traces its origins to the prehistoric era. The man is the protector but the woman has to know that. Should she harbor any skepticism regarding your willingness to defend her, you shall promptly forfeit any sense of affinity or alignment she may have felt towards you.

Superman serves as a prime illustration of ideal masculinity. Clark Kent possesses inherently masculine traits at his essence, yet he does not embody this role outwardly as Clark Kent, thereby eluding Lois Lane's recognition of him as a potential love interest. Clark can truly embody his masculine identity only when he grants himself the authorization to embrace his transformation into Superman. Lois, alongside every other individual present, observes his aura of confidence and commanding presence. This is also applicable in the context of Spiderman.

It is evident that one does not require superhuman abilities to accomplish this task. During the same Tony Robbins event, I had the opportunity to observe an individual exhibiting a more feminine disposition in an otherwise masculine demeanor. He appeared to embrace a more peaceful and nonviolent ideology, resembling a pacifist or a gentle soul who was consciously mindful of avoiding any disruptions or conflicts. He and his significant other were experiencing difficulties and he was unsure about the cause. Following an extensive line of inquiry, it became apparent that he exhibited behavior indicative of someone who felt disempowered. He formerly excelled in rugby until sustaining a knee injury, which ultimately compelled him to cease participation. When discussing his involvement in rugby, his countenance ignited with enthusiasm and exuded a profound sense of pride and self-assurance, reflecting an unwavering belief in his ability to outperform any opponent on the rugby field. Tony inquired whether the gentleman possessed the ability to outperform him in a game of rugby, to which the individual emphatically affirmed, "certainly!" (It's worth noting that Tony's stature exceeded that of the aforementioned person by at least a foot.) Notably, the latter displayed unwavering resolve and refused to yield in any manner. That is presence. That is confidence. He had assumed a commanding presence during our interaction, displaying a newfound sense of masculine authority that was palpable. It was awesome!

As an individual of the male gender, it is essential to engage in activities that instill a sense of empowerment within oneself. Virtually every male protagonist depicted in films or tales is characterized by their strong and traditionally masculine traits. All those men whom women find incredibly captivating possess inherent qualities of confidence and masculinity. I strongly urge you to be mindful of the encompassing presence of this situation. Please exercise caution in this regard before you exit your residence or engage in any form of visual entertainment.

When I use the phrase 'give yourself permission,' I am referring to a specific scenario involving an individual who, as exemplified in the previous anecdote, held the belief that he needed to adopt a calm and amicable demeanor in order to please others. However, it was not until the topic of rugby emerged in conversation that he finally allowed himself to embrace his innate confidence and assertiveness, which the sport naturally awakened within him.

"Below are a number of actions you can undertake to enhance your sense of masculinity:

take martial arts

Obtain a punching bag.

Defend yourself and assert your rights

Do not allow yourself to be demeaned by anyone, regardless of their standing or influence. (A lack of assertiveness garners little respect.)

Engage in a strategic and decisive action to cultivate an unwavering sense of confidence and determination, commonly referred to as entering a highly focused and optimal mental state.

Maintain an upright posture by keeping your shoulders aligned and your chin raised while walking, sitting, and standing. This conscious adjustment in body position will rapidly influence your emotional state.

Engage in leisure activities with male acquaintances who partake in stereotypical masculine pursuits.

If it wasn't already apparent, I am an avid admirer of Tony Robbins. I have successfully traversed a path of burning embers with temperatures reaching 2,000 degrees on three separate occasions. The method employed by Tony to facilitate 6,000 individuals traversing hot coals involves inducing them into a particular mental and emotional state. One can enter a state of mind by recollecting a moment in which one experienced invincibility. Possibly, you achieved a remarkable success or any other accomplishment that made you feel exceedingly empowered. Tony instructs you to repeatedly amplify the intensity by vocally exclaiming "YES!" and simultaneously executing a forceful gesture, such as striking your chest or performing a punch-like motion. After engaging in this task repeatedly, one experiences a sense of invincibility and a sensation of bodily vibration. It is a remarkable sensation.

You can easily achieve this 'condition' by executing your power move within a matter of seconds. If you possess a heightened sense of empowerment to the extent that you could confidently traverse scorching hot coals, you would no longer allow trivial matters such as the actions of an individual who derides you at the workplace to have any impact on your emotional state. You shall regain your authority, and this will mark the final instance in which you endure such circumstances. He would discern from your mere presence that you have reached a state of satiety. Do not permit anyone to disempower you, whether it be through self-doubt or others, including women.

Acknowledge Your Preconceived Notion Of An Idealized Version Of Love And Free Yourself From Its Constraints.

Each of us holds a conceptualization of what we perceive love to ideally entail. This representation is influenced by our familial connections, interpersonal relationships, acquaintances, societal norms, cultural values, media portrayal, and the global community as a whole.

As we mature and engage in romantic partnerships, it is inherent for us to seek in our companions the embodiment of our conceptualization of love.

The apprehension of potentially falling short of attaining such an ideal, of facing disappointment in love (our self-centered conception of love), entices us to forsake our authentic selves, to assume a façade and engage in the performance we believe is necessary for social acceptance and affection. Engaging in such behavior is incompatible with self-love.

The word "fear" has its origins in Old English, where it originally meant "danger, peril, ambush, and snare." Its fundamental sense was that of a "trap." Additionally, it is etymologically connected to the Greek term "pera," which means "to go through," as well as the English word "fare," which means "to go." These connections suggest an underlying significance of "what one undergoes or experiences." In contemporary usage, one of the meanings of "fear" is "to anticipate something with apprehension or uncertainty."

The apprehension regarding unfulfilled romantic expectations leads to emotional distress. The apprehension of suffering and the inclination to evade it may lead one to be enticed into manipulating another's affections.

This can be accomplished by conveying to them what you perceive as their desired narrative, or by projecting an idealized version of yourself that aligns with their expectations in order to garner their affection. I designate this phenomenon as the Seductress Syndrome, which encompasses not solely romantic associations, but also all interpersonal connections and one's aspirations for personal gain within them.

Rather than succumbing to this pitfall, it is imperative that you acquire the ability to consistently embrace your authentic self and allow those individuals who do not genuinely care for you to dissipate. The anticipation of someone meeting your conception of love will invariably result in anguish.

The concept of expectation originates from the Latin term 'expectare,' which is derived from the combination of 'ex' (meaning out) and 'spectare' (meaning to look). When you hold certain expectations, you are actively monitoring or anticipating its occurrence. When one imposes a certain expectation upon an individual, such as one's personal conception of love, they are seeking fulfillment from the other party (external to oneself).

Disappointment, in its etymological roots, signified the act of being deprived of an appointment or not fulfilling a scheduled commitment, serving as the precursor to its contemporary meaning of failing to meet an expectation and causing frustration.

I kindly request your consideration of the notion that seeking fulfillment of your romantic ideals from another individual can ultimately lead to personal disappointment. You are failing to meet with your ultimate life partner or destined companion, who represents the unparalleled realization of the profound spiritual connection with the divine within yourself.

Pain carries an etymological significance rooted in the concept of retribution, derived from the Latin word 'pen' meaning 'penalty', which also yielded the term 'pine'. Initially, pain denoted distress or suffering. You inflict distress upon yourself by desperately yearning for another person to meet your idealized standards of affection.

Suffering ensues from seeking fulfillment externally. It is imperative to acknowledge that the source of your disappointment in desiring someone else to meet your expectations lies within yourself, as you impose your personal ideals upon them.

Suffering arises from the tendency to have certain expectations of others, rather than accepting them for who they truly are. If one desires to cultivate affection from others, there is a need to grant them the freedom to express their authentic selves without any preconceived notions or demands. Ultimately, is that not the desired outcome one seeks in a prospective companion?

In the event that you decline to reveal your authentic self, how can one truly embrace and appreciate you as an individual, accepting and cherishing you for who you truly are? If one is unable to embrace and permit an individual to express their genuine self, it becomes implausible to anticipate their reciprocation of affection towards oneself. They will develop feelings of resentment towards you instead.

Anticipating that your significant other will meet your personal expectations will inevitably lead to the dissolution of any relationship. Placing your expectations on another person is not only unfair but also devoid of genuine love; it is an act of selfishness, unequivocally speaking.

Engaging in this behavior implies a failure to exhibit the Unconditional Love that you, yourself, desire from others. Once more, it is posited that the Law of

Attraction, also referred to as the Law of Love, maintains that similar actions are inclined to draw similar actions. One shall consistently receive based on the effort and contributions exerted.

We hold mutual expectations of one another perpetually, often without conscious awareness. Upon acknowledging this behavior within oneself, it becomes incumbent upon that individual to cease this conduct and provide assistance to others in doing likewise.

Exemplify leadership by providing a secure environment where individuals can freely express their genuine emotions without fear of criticism, envy, reproach, hostility, or concern for the expected outcome.

One can only proffer genuine affection when one does not require others to conform to anything other than their authentic selves. This signifies an unwavering affection, and represents the true essence of releasing something you cherish.

One's affection for another is not authentic if they cannot accept and embrace their innate essence. The converse holds true as well. If an individual impedes your authentic expression, it indicates that their love towards you is not genuine. Rather, they are imposing their misguided notions of love upon you, displaying a sense of self-centeredness.

Having a genuine understanding of love entails demonstrating its essence through acts of selflessness and generosity. It is imperative for you to cultivate the ability to perceive things in their true form, rather than through the lens of your personal preferences or desires. It is imperative that you cease the practice of molding yourself according to perceived expectations and desires of others. It is thus advisable to focus on discovering and embracing your genuine self.

Genuine sincerity is imperative in discovering and actualizing the true purpose of your existence, the innermost longing of your heart, which shall ultimately bestow upon you genuine affection and enduring bliss. This necessitates a perpetual commitment to embracing your emotions and articulating them devoid of anger, condemnation, fault-finding, aggression, or anticipation.

Avoid suppressing or negating your emotions; rather, express them truthfully and candidly, without the need to justify or seek forgiveness for having them.

One must attain a stage where they are capable of confronting and encountering their desires, while also being able to relinquish them in the event that maintaining a grip on said desires leads to a betrayal of their authentic self.

The practice of embodying authenticity and approaching life in accordance with the principles of reciprocity will ultimately guide you towards genuine self-discovery, self-acceptance, finding your true partner in life, achieving prosperity and stability, fulfilling your life's calling, and attaining any other prerequisites for personal contentment that you may seek.

Acquiring proficiency in this matter may necessitate a substantial amount of dedication and perseverance, coupled with the likelihood of encountering obstacles that may jeopardize one's integrity. Nevertheless, it is imperative that one remains resolute and unyielding in the face of adversity. In due course, it will ultimately guide you towards your intended destination, affording you the opportunity to reflect upon the challenging trials and tribulations, thus prompting gratitude and understanding of their purpose. You would not exchange it for anything else.

Conclusion

I can only provide a limited amount of information and offer guidance regarding the qualities to seek in a prospective partner. In all truthfulness, it is imperative that every individual possesses their own checklist. Certainly, we all desire an individual who possesses qualities such as kindness, compassion, intelligence, physical attractiveness, and financial stability, to name just a few aspects that could be indefinitely expanded upon. Simply state that you possess an individual who possesses all of these qualities. Are you done? You possess a unique set of qualities that make you exceptional in your individual manner. I can envision that you possess idiosyncrasies. You must find someone to love your quirks and they will have their individual quirks that you should love too. In contemporary society, individuals tend to either enter into matrimonial unions or become unintentionally entangled with their respective partners due to various circumstances. It appears that there is a collective propensity towards hastening matrimonial unions or experiencing distress at the prospect of being solitary. Finding a suitable partner can be a challenging endeavor for young women, and it is important not to rush into such a significant decision. Anything that is hastily done lacks a solid basis and is prone to easy collapse. It will come naturally. It is imperative that whomever you encounter demonstrates a genuine affection towards your authentic self. While this notion may appear simplistic, it remains profoundly accurate. The sole means by which you can acquire this knowledge necessitates a deliberate allocation of your time. Time is the sole verity that manifests inherently. Mutual adoration between the two of you is expected. To the extent that a bond exists that is impervious to rupture. It is imperative for the experience to be both organic and unforced. Both of you should perpetually embody the exhilarating affection reminiscent of youthful ardor, with the only gauge of time being the reflection witnessed in the looking glass.

Any individual who possesses affection towards you ought to exhibit unconditional love towards you. He ought to be prepared to enter into a romantic partnership. He should know this. This deduction should not be necessary. It should not be necessary to exert such a significant amount of effort to rectify his condition or your respective circumstances, or, to compound matters, his own predicament. This implies that you should disengage in order to avoid squandering your valuable time and, most significantly, your emotions. Tears ought to exclusively manifest in response to joy rather than sorrow.

Does he possess the necessary qualifications to provide care for you? That does not imply that you should be readily available to cater to their every need. However, do his characteristics sufficiently equip him to handle you in your vulnerable state?

It is imperative to carefully assess various aspects of a relationship, despite outward appearances or assertions from the other person concerning their commitment level. Points to be taken into consideration are whether he is prepared. One must acknowledge that men have the capacity to experience emotions, particularly when transitioning from a previous romantic partnership. This represents the manifestation of feminine energy from his previous experiences manifested in his present state. Initially, this might appear attractive to you since it is uncommon for men to candidly acknowledge their desire for a committed partnership. The emergence of this feminine energy will inevitably manifest in a sense of neediness, which may lead to a diminished sense of attraction on your part. Gradually, you will come to understand the reasons behind his previous partner's decision to end their relationship.

If you are currently perusing this, it suggests that you are seeking a long-term individual. Effective communication is essential. Do both of you possess a shared understanding and communicate with similar styles? Do you comprehend the intended message even in seemingly uncomplicated forms of communication such as text messages? Do you struggle? Small actions can have a significant impact.

He can exert the necessary effort if he engages in the process of comprehending your true nature. You are a work in progress. Consequently, will you extend the same courtesy to him? Does it hold value in your perspective?

In contemporary times, it is observed that men exhibit a tendency to enter into relationships at a similar pace as women. The primary justification is our requirement for consistent sexual activity. Therefore, our focus lies on the short term rather than the long term. Sad but true. In a romantic partnership, it is essential for a man to possess a comprehensive set of qualities and characteristics. While wealth is not a prerequisite, it is imperative that he embodies the qualities of a truly captivating and ideal partner, your own personal Prince Charming. Despite the fact that some men may come with emotional baggage from past relationships, their presence should not be a concern if they are fully committed to you. Nobody is perfect. The responsibility for ensuring its perfection lies with both of you.

It is abundantly clear to me when composing this piece. An individual should be responsible for meeting your requirements, thus eliminating the need to seek fulfillment elsewhere. The crux of the matter lies in one thing: happiness. True happiness originates from a singular source, one that resides within the bonds of familial relationships. The foundation of the family begins within the household. When all elements are aligned harmoniously within one's household, external concerns cease to perturb, as the prospect of returning to a comforting haven provides a source of solace and anticipation. Your spouse. Your closest companion, your trusted confidante, your romantic partner. This is the stage at which a relationship flourishes.

Whomever has an affection for you ought to strive for their utmost potential at present. Consequently, he is capable of giving his utmost effort in the relationship. Both of you should contribute some form of value or expertise to the discussion or project at hand. This method provides the most optimal approach to commence. If he remains entangled within his own inner struggles, what capacity does he possess to serve you?

Although it may seem like I am digressing, there lies a kernel of truth when one carefully examines the matter. Research indicates that Jewish couples exhibit significantly lower divorce rates when compared to couples of diverse religious backgrounds. It is evident as to why this is the case. Every individual, upon entering the institution of marriage, recites their vows in the presence of a solemnized officiant. According to research, when it comes to the Jewish population, they take an additional stride that significantly impacts the outcome.

In adherence to Jewish custom, it is expected that the husband shall demonstrate a genuine love for his wife, treating her with utmost respect and placing her needs and well-being above his own. (Tractate Sota 47a) Moreover, a husband who dutifully fulfills his responsibilities shall be deserving of a harmonious domestic environment. (Yevamoth 62b). One cannot refute the immense impact possessed by both of those sentences.

Jewish men solemnly pledge and execute a contractual agreement to fulfill the needs of their spouses. They pledge to uphold two significant factors within the context of the relationship.

The foremost duty he must uphold is to respect and fulfill his obligations towards his wife. Having the capability to provide her with the essential necessities, such as a comfortable dwelling, sustenance, attire, and demonstrating thoughtfulness by showering her with tokens of affection, so as to cultivate a fulfilling marital bond. He must possess the capability to fulfill her sexual desires.

The second scenario pertains to any unforeseen circumstances within the relationship which may lead to either a divorce or the unfortunate event of death. He has a legal obligation to provide her with a monetary settlement.

Negotiation of properties is also available within the terms and conditions of this contract. This could be deemed as potentially the most ancient manifestation of a prenuptial agreement. With the presence of both factors within the context of the relationship. He undoubtedly approaches the relationship with a profound sense of earnestness due to his acute awareness of the potential consequences at stake. He would be inclined to devote additional effort to it in the event of adversity rather than abandoning it. This item serves as a comforting aid for women, providing a sense of security and peace of mind. Having the awareness that he is committed for a significant duration rather than solely seeking immediate gains. It is a solemn agreement to uphold his commitment to his spouse. I am not suggesting that you specifically seek out a Jewish gentleman, but rather a man who embodies and embraces these core principles. By doing so, you will find a suitable partner of exceptional character. Females possess inherent emotional depth and demonstrate commitment to sustaining a relationship despite enduring distressing circumstances. Males are prone to promptly pursue fresh opportunities when they arise.

It is quite heartwarming to witness elderly couples strolling side by side, reminiscent of young school children, and occasionally displaying affection through tender hand-holding or the infrequent exchange of kisses when parting ways. It is expected that all individuals strive to attain such qualities/attributes. This is the driving force behind global dynamics. It serves as evidence that the essence of romance persists, patiently awaiting our embrace. Each individual possesses a unique person who awaits them in a specific location. It shall arrive, but you must place your trust in its arrival. Energy encompasses all aspects of our existence. Release the sense of desperation and longing for a romantic connection, and instead cultivate a state of joy and satisfaction. A romantic partnership will promptly ensue.

One of the songs that I hold dear is penned by Jack Jones, titled "Wives and Lovers," and it was composed in the year 1961. I would highly recommend that individuals avail themselves the opportunity to listen to it. You have been transported to an era characterized by its simplicity, integrity, and traditional expressions of love. The refrain is "Wives ought to also act as lovers." Seek refuge in his embrace upon his return to your presence. The aforementioned statement may appear to contain underlying gender biases, yet upon listening to the song, the intended meaning becomes clear. It is incumbent upon a gentleman to meet his responsibilities towards his lady, just as it is expected of a lady to reciprocate in kind. Ensuring that you both have a genuine sense of identity. Establishing solid foundations in the relationship instills a sense of assurance, thus inspiring future generations to strive for excellence.

www.ingramcontent.com/pod-product-compliance
Lightning Source LLC
Chambersburg PA
CBHW050026130526
44590CB00042B/1968